Teaching Grammar through Literature

This essential guide offers a fresh approach to integrating grammar effectively into the classroom as a vital strand of English that both enlivens and enriches students' understanding of literature. It aims to demystify grammar and empower teachers with the knowledge, inspiration and practical ideas to confidently teach grammar to students at any stage of their secondary education. The authors demonstrate that routinely weaving grammar into lessons and the study of literature, rather than teaching it as an abstract set of rules, enables students to see grammar in a more flexible, enjoyable and exciting way.

Each chapter clearly defines complex terminology and provides an essential overview of relevant subject knowledge. With multiple examples of textual analysis and a variety of adaptable lesson plans for popular Key Stage 3 and Key Stage 4 texts, the book shows how grammatical requirements can be taught in a lively, literature-based manner, developing students' understanding and improving the quality of their creative and academic writing. Taught like this, grammar becomes a decoding tool: a key to unlocking deeper meaning within texts that enriches the reading experience.

Considering a wide range of texts, *Teaching Grammar through Literature* thoroughly works through core grammatical concepts such as:

- sentences and sentence clauses
- nouns
- verbs
- determiners
- punctuation
- extension vocabulary.

This book is a source of fresh and exciting ideas for all practising secondary school English teachers. It will revolutionise teaching and enrich students' understanding of literature and the grammatical theory within.

Rachel Fenn is Head of English at École Jeannine Manuel in London, UK.

Anna McGlynn is Deputy Head of English at Weald of Kent Grammar School, UK.

Teaching Grammar through Literature

Bringing Language to Life in the Secondary Classroom

Rachel Fenn and Anna McGlynn

LONDON AND NEW YORK

First published 2018
by Routledge
2 Park Square, Milton Park, Abingdon, Oxon OX14 4RN

and by Routledge
711 Third Avenue, New York, NY 10017

Routledge is an imprint of the Taylor & Francis Group, an informa business

© 2018 Rachel Fenn and Anna McGlynn

The right of Rachel Fenn and Anna McGlynn to be identified as authors of this work has been asserted by them in accordance with sections 77 and 78 of the Copyright, Designs and Patents Act 1988.

All rights reserved. No part of this book may be reprinted or reproduced or utilised in any form or by any electronic, mechanical, or other means, now known or hereafter invented, including photocopying and recording, or in any information storage or retrieval system, without permission in writing from the publishers.

Trademark notice: Product or corporate names may be trademarks or registered trademarks, and are used only for identification and explanation without intent to infringe.

British Library Cataloguing-in-Publication Data
A catalogue record for this book is available from the British Library

Library of Congress Cataloging-in-Publication Data
Names: Fenn, Rachel, author. | McGlynn, Anna, author.
Title: Teaching grammar through literature : bringing language to life in the secondary classroom / Rachel Fenn and Anna McGlynn.
Description: Abingdon, Oxon ; New York, NY : Routledge is an imprint of the Taylor & Francis Group, an Informa Business, [2018] | Includes bibliographical references and index.
Identifiers: LCCN 2017041498 (print) | LCCN 2017060649 (ebook) | ISBN 9780203732939 (ebook) | ISBN 9781138300996 (hbk) | ISBN 9781138301009 (pbk) | ISBN 9780203732939 (ebk)
Subjects: LCSH: English language—Grammar—Study and teaching (Secondary)
Classification: LCC LB1631 (ebook) | LCC LB1631 .F46 2018 (print) | DDC 428.0071/2—dc23
LC record available at https://lccn.loc.gov/2017041498

ISBN: 978-1-138-30099-6 (hbk)
ISBN: 978-1-138-30100-9 (pbk)
ISBN: 978-0-203-73293-9 (ebk)

Typeset in Melior
by Keystroke, Neville Lodge, Tettenhall, Wolverhampton

Contents

	Introduction	1
1	Sentences and sentence clauses	4
2	Nouns	21
3	Verbs	39
4	Determiners	60
5	Punctuation	71
6	Extension vocabulary (or 'wow' words!)	87
7	Activity A–Z	112
	Bibliography	117
	Index	119

Introduction

Grammar is a topic that tends to fill both teachers and students alike with fear and boredom. As many English teachers are literature, rather than language, specialists, teaching the complexities of grammatical concepts can sometimes feel like an impossible challenge. There is a twofold issue here: teachers may not be clear in their own understanding of how to explain the fundamentals of English grammar, it being a largely instinctive rather than learned knowledge base, and from this lack of understanding comes a difficulty in being able to apply grammatical knowledge to the analysis of literature and the teaching of writing. This book aims to address both of these areas, giving English teachers a clear explanation of the grammatical terminology they need to be able to teach their students, as well as a step-by-step guide to how this knowledge can be applied to the analysis of commonly taught texts across all three key stages.

The priority of this book is to demystify grammar and demonstrate to English teachers that the teaching of grammar can be both enjoyable and incredibly beneficial in enabling students to better identify meaning in texts as well as improve the quality of their own creative and academic writing. We believe the key to this is an integral approach to teaching grammar; rather than delivering discrete 'grammar lessons', grammar should be routinely woven into lessons where its application can be immediately applied and practised. Studying grammar as an abstract concept may give children the theory, but in our experience it does not help them understand how to actually apply this theory in practice. Through giving examples of textual analysis and ideas as to how lessons can be based around particular grammatical concepts, this book will provide teachers with an essential tool to help integrate grammar effectively into their classrooms as a vital strand of English that enlivens and enriches students' understanding of literature.

At Key Stage 3, many students will already have benefited from the increase in the teaching of grammatical concepts in Key Stage 2. By the time they leave primary school, students will now be expected to have a secure grasp of all types of punctuation, be able to identify the name and function of words within a sentence, and name and identify the full range of sentence clauses, explaining how these can be used for effect. Students will be familiar with a vast range of grammatical terminology, such as determiners, fronted adverbials, relative and possessive pronouns, subordinate clauses and modal verbs, some of which may be unfamiliar to – and even induce terror in – English teachers who have not themselves been taught grammar. It is our job as secondary English teachers to capitalise on the knowledge our primary colleagues have given the students who join us in Year 7, and enable these students to develop their existing knowledge by showing them how to apply it to the analysis and construction of increasingly complex texts. Particularly at Key Stage 3, which naturally has a greater focus on creative rather than academic writing, grammatical knowledge can be used to allow students to make more thoughtful, deliberate decisions about the ordering of their words, punctuation and sentence clauses, leading to more sophisticated pieces of work. Freeing grammar from the constraints of something that is taught to enable students to write 'correctly' is key here; it is crucial for teachers to understand that grammar is not solely about accuracy, but about enabling a fluency of style. The more confident teachers are with grammatical terminology, the more creative they can be in moving beyond merely showing students what grammatical correctness looks like. They will instead begin to focus on how grammatical constructions can be manipulated to enhance the beauty of the sentences students create.

At Key Stage 4, where the analysis of language becomes the focus of English lessons as students begin to prepare for GCSE examinations, grammar can often fall by the wayside as themes, characters, symbols and context take over discussions of texts. However, a sound knowledge of grammatical terminology is now a vital element of the new strengthened Literature GCSE syllabi, with assessment objective two (AO2) in most exam boards focusing on the craft and intention of the author, an assessment objective that continues at A Level. As such, students need to be able to look at texts at word level, considering how sentences are constructed for effect and what this adds to the interpretation of meaning. Understanding more complex grammatical terms such as lexis, semantic field, metonymy and antimetabole, alongside being able to discuss the role of more simple grammatical structures such as possessive pronouns and sentence clauses, will be key to meeting the demands of the new curriculum. Being able to apply these terms to texts will add a more sophisticated layer of analysis and interpretation to students' responses and enable them to make more evaluative comments about the authors' intentions. Teachers need to be able to identify these concepts as well as discuss their purpose, and, with many of these terms previously not being discussed until much later in a student's academic career, some teachers may not be familiar with the variety of potential grammatical terms that can be applied. Especially as many of the texts on the literature syllabus are new at Key Stage 4, with the additional focus on nineteenth century texts brought in from 2016, the chapters in this book will provide a considerable amount of support by demonstrating how grammatical terms can be used to fruitfully analyse older and more complex texts such as *Great Expectations* and *Jane Eyre*. There will also be examples of Shakespeare, modern plays and poetry alongside ways to approach unseen text practice, another key feature of the new Key Stage 4 curriculum.

At Key Stage 5, the demands of A Level continue to require a sound knowledge of grammatical structures as part of AO2 for most examination boards. Students must be able to comment on how a writer uses language and structure to create meaning and they will be expected to be able to use advanced grammatical terminology to both identify and explain features within texts. When teaching students at A Level, teachers will often be grappling with more complex, antiquated and non-traditional texts that require knowledge of obscure terms. We will discuss terminology such as metonymy and synaesthesia in order to demonstrate how an understanding of these challenging concepts can take textual analysis to a more demanding level, enabling students to make subtle interpretations of authors' intentions when considering their linguistic and structural choices. We will look at a range of commonly studied novels, plays and poems across several syllabi to show the application of advanced grammatical analysis in practice.

Overall, what this book aims to do is empower teachers with the knowledge, inspiration and practical ideas to confidently teach grammar relevantly to students at any stage of their secondary education. Feeding an understanding of grammar naturally into the study of literature, rather than teaching it as an abstract set of rules, enables students to see grammar in a more flexible and exciting way. Taught like this, grammar becomes a decoding tool: a key to unlocking deeper meaning within texts that enriches the reading experience. Whether you are already confident with grammar or not, we hope this book will be a source of fresh and inspiring ideas that will revolutionise your teaching and open your students' eyes to the many wonders of the English language.

Sentences and sentence clauses

Most students should feel confident in being able to identify different types of simple sentences and sentence clauses. Students coming into Key Stage 3 from UK primary schools will have been taught about compound, simple and complex sentences, as well as main and subordinate clauses, and should be able to clearly identify these in practice. However, in-depth understanding of the actual function and effect of these varying constructions can present more of a challenge. Many students may not know that clauses can be split into finer, more grammatically descriptive categories, or why a compound sentence might have been used over a simple sentence beyond being able to say that it makes the sentence more 'interesting' or 'informative'. Understanding the effects of different sentence choices will enable students to make more precise and insightful comments about a writer's craft. This can also lead to students making more thoughtful decisions about the way in which they construct their own creative or analytical sentences for effect.

In this chapter we will break down the different sentence types and clauses, clearly explaining how they can be identified and used for effect, with extracts from popularly studied texts across all three Key Stages to evidence how analysis of sentence construction can work in practice. We will also look at how sentences and sentence clauses can be woven into the teaching of creative writing, helping students to make more informed, deliberate choices to develop the sophistication of their work.

In all of our grammatical explanations we strive to simplify and clarify as much as possible and opt for the most straightforward approach when explaining terminology. There are always ways in which grammatical constructs can be broken down into more finite technical explanations, but as our students are not required to be linguistic experts we feel that too much terminology can often be a hindrance rather than a help. As such, we have included only the terms that we feel will actually be of use to students of secondary school age.

Main clause

Every deliberately grammatically correct sentence should include at least one main clause. In its simplest and most straightforward terms, **a main clause consists of a subject and a predicate** and **stands alone as a complete sentence.** The **subject will** typically be a noun, noun phrase or pronoun, and the **predicate will be a verb or verb phrase**. As such, the sentence *I ate dinner last night* serves as a main clause just as *I ate* does, with the 'I' in both cases functioning as the subject and the verb 'ate' functioning as the predicate.

Note: some students may have been taught that a main clause is called an 'independent clause'.

Subordinate clause

The subordinate clause is the part of the sentence that **does not stand alone,** and should, in a grammatically correct sentence, be **joined to a main clause either through the use of punctuation or a conjunction. Subordinate clauses begin with either a relative pronoun or a subordinate conjunction.** They will still contain a subject and a verb but will not make sense by themselves. *Who arrived late thanks to the tube strike* is an example of a subordinate clause beginning with a relative pronoun (who). This is clearly a subordinate clause as we are missing the vital information of knowing to whom the relative pronoun refers. *After she had written the book* is an example of a subordinate clause beginning with a subordinate conjunction (after); again, this is clearly a subordinate clause as we have no idea of the context the 'after' is referring to. A subordinate clause can come anywhere within a sentence; it is not always at the end.

Note: some students may have been taught that the subordinate clause is called a 'dependent' clause.

A subordinate clause has two main categories, usually being either conditional or relative. A conditional clause describes something that is possible or probable, and a relative clause gives more information on a topic and is identified as beginning with a relative pronoun. **Relative clauses can be restrictive or non-restrictive**; a restrictive relative clause gives necessary information about the noun that comes before it, and a non-restrictive relative clause gives non-necessary information about a noun that comes before it. For example:

She showed him the painting that he had bought.

'That he had bought' functions here as a **restrictive relative clause** as it gives necessary information about the painting and is introduced by a relative pronoun.

His hand was cut by the knife, which he was using to chop up the meat.

'Which he was using to chop up the meat' functions here as a **non-restrictive relative clause** because we don't need to know what he was doing with the knife in order to know that his hand was cut.

I can't come to the party unless my mum can drive me.

'Unless my mum can drive me' functions here as a **conditional clause** as it details an event that can only happen if something else happens first.

Simple sentence

A simple sentence is simply a **main clause:** a sentence with a single subject and a single verb. For example:

I ate dinner.
Sam was running late for school.
There were only five people in the queue.

Compound sentence

A compound sentence is made up of **two main clauses, or simple sentences, joined by a conjunction**. For example:

I ate dinner and it was delicious.

Complex sentence

A complex sentence contains **a main and a subordinate clause joined by a subordinating conjunction or punctuation**. For example:

She turned up, late as usual, to the lesson.
As it careered around the bend, the bus tottered onto two wheels.

Sentences of any construction can be split into four main categories:

Declarative

A declarative sentence is one that makes a statement. It will give information or ideas. Declarative sentences are the basis of most speech and writing. *There was no possibility of taking a walk that day*, the famous opening line of Charlotte Brontë's *Jane Eyre*, is a declarative sentence.

Imperative

An imperative sentence is one that gives a command or a request. Some imperative sentences can also be exclamatory, depending on the context, such as *Stop*! Other imperative sentences – such as *please can you pick up that pen?* – can seem to be interrogative questions, but the difference between an imperative and an interrogative is that an interrogative sentence is asking a question, not making a request.

Exclamatory

An exclamatory sentence expresses strong emotion and always uses exclamation marks. These sorts of sentences can often be headache-inducing for us teachers when students feel the need to make every sentence, regardless of how exciting the content, end in an exclamation mark or, even worse, the dreaded several exclamation marks. To save yourself from this frustration, make sure your students understand that they only need to use an exclamation mark when there is strong emotion involved. *I can't believe I just won a million pounds!* definitely needs an exclamation mark: *I went shopping and bought some shoes!* does not.

Interrogative

Interrogative sentences always ask a direct question and always end in a question mark. As explained above, these can be confused with imperative sentences, where a request is being made, so ensure that students understand what a direct question looks like. For example:

Did she wear the red dress?
Have you eaten yet?

Putting it into practice

Now we've covered the basics of the theory behind sentence construction, we're going to have a look at how this works in practice when it comes to exploring how texts have been constructed and what meanings we can infer from this. We have split our examples by Key Stage to enable you to see a variety of texts and levels of analysis.

 ## Key Stage 3: *Northern Lights* by Philip Pullman

Extract from Chapter One

"Lyra! What the hell are you doing?"
"Let go of me and I'll tell you!"
"I'll break your arm first. How dare you come in here?"
"I've just saved your life!"
They were still for a moment, the girl twisted in pain but grimacing to prevent herself from crying out louder, the man bent over her frowning like thunder.

(London: Scholastic, 1998, p.14)

For Key Stage 3 students studying a text, character is often the focus of discussion. As such, looking at characters and how they speak is usually the easiest way for students to start to feel confident at using grammar in their analysis of texts.

> **WHY NOT CONSIDER?**
>
> - How could you use sentence types to draw comparisons between the characters?
> - What is interesting about the type of sentences Lyra and Lord Asriel use to address each other? What could this infer about their relationship?
> - How could knowledge of grammatical vocabulary enable younger students to make more insightful literary analysis?

Here the most effective way of looking at sentence structure is to consider what it tells us about the characters of Lyra and Lord Asriel. Let's tackle Lord Asriel first. We can tell much about his character from this short section of dialogue solely by looking at the sentence construction. Lord Asriel's first line, *"Lyra! What the hell are you doing?"* uses two simple sentences: a one word, exclamatory sentence, followed by an interrogative. His next line of dialogue, *"I'll break your arm first. How dare you come in here?"* consists of two more simple sentences, the first a declarative and the following an interrogative. Lord Asriel's speech is therefore made up of short, perfunctory sentences that demand answers of Lyra. By using interrogatives he places himself in a position of power and authority. He has the right to ask questions, and Lyra does not. The fact that his sentences are simple shows a direct, no-nonsense, powerful personality; he is someone who is used to being in charge and who has no need to impress with the language he uses.

Lyra's responses to Lord Asriel are interesting. She uses one simple and one compound sentence, but both are exclamatory. Like her father, Lyra uses simple, straightforward sentence constructions; she sees no need to waste time or effort on impressing with her language. Her use of exclamation shows her anger and frustration at her treatment, and the fact that she responds to interrogative questions with exclamatory rather than declarative sentences hints at a rebellious nature; she is resisting the attempts of Lord Asriel to control her through refusing to reply in the expected manner.

The similarities between Lyra and Lord Asriel's sentence construction reveal shared character traits of confidence and a desire to be in control, while also revealing the power struggle in their relationship; Lyra will not submit to Lord Asriel and so they are in conflict from their very first encounter. This could, for more able students, be a way to introduce the idea of foreshadowing; it can be argued that Pullman foreshadows the revelation of Lord Asriel's true identity as Lyra's biological father through the similarities in their speech at their first meeting.

As we have shown, grammatical analysis of the construction of sentences can already reveal a great deal before attention is turned to their actual word-level content. Students can use their knowledge of different types of sentences to draw interesting conclusions about characters' personalities and motivations that can greatly enrich their understanding of a character's role within the text.

We would suggest that this type of activity is best used with a short piece of text, with students taught only the terms they need to know to be able to analyse the sentences effectively. Here a knowledge of main and subordinate clauses, simple, compound and complex sentences and the four categories of sentence types is all that is needed, and much of this should only need to be refreshed rather than taught from scratch. A textual analysis activity like this can easily be differentiated for a range of confidence levels. For students who are less confident, they can achieve success through correctly identifying the different types of sentences in the extract. They can then be helped to a more thoughtful answer by being able to see that Lyra is not answering Lord Asriel's questions, and exploring what this might tell us about Lyra's character. More confident students should be able to draw out what can be inferred from the similarities between Lyra and Lord Asriel's speech, with the most confident being able to think about ideas of power, control and foreshadowing through the sentence types used.

Key Stage 4: *Jane Eyre* by Charlotte Brontë

Extract from Chapter One

There was no possibility of taking a walk that day. We had been wandering, indeed, in the leafless shrubbery an hour in the morning; but since dinner (Mrs Reed, when there was no company, dined early) the cold winter wind had brought with it clouds so sombre, and a rain so penetrating, that further out-door exercise was now out of the question.

(London: Penguin, 2006, p.9)

At Key Stage 4, students can use grammar as the basis for some more in-depth and subtle interpretative comments than can be demanded of Key Stage 3 students. Both character and theme can be drawn on when discussing sentence structure here, as well as context. As can be seen from this extract, the sentence structure is non-standard, using what we would now consider to be incorrect grammar. This provides the opportunity to discuss the context of nineteenth century English in that there was, as of yet, no standardised punctuation, and writers were freer to be more creative in the ways in which they separated sentence clauses.

> **WHY NOT CONSIDER?**
>
> - How does the sentence construction reflect Jane's status, role and state of mind?
> - How could context be involved in the discussion of the use of sentence construction?
> - What conclusions might be drawn about Jane's character when looking at the contrast between simple and complex sentences?

The opening to *Jane Eyre* begins with a simple declarative sentence: *'There was no possibility of taking a walk that day.'* This is followed by a complex sentence with a number of interesting features. There is a conditional clause, three conjunctions, plus a compound sentence inserted in brackets within the subordinate clause. This is a lengthy, highly complex sentence construction consisting of a large amount of information, not all of which is necessary. In fact the simple, declarative opening sentence tells us everything the second, much more complex, sentence does; the entire second sentence is arguably superfluous to the text. What meaning could we infer from this sentence construction? Character-wise, this offers us an intriguing insight into Jane Eyre's personality. There is an element of straight-forwardness about her; her first sentence is simple, uncluttered, entirely declamatory, as befitting a governess who is used to teaching simple facts to small children. However, the second sentence reveals an outpouring of unnecessary information, constructed through several clauses, suggesting a mind teeming with knowledge that Jane is desperate to express. It can be argued that this simple, followed by complex, construction reflects the act of teaching: giving knowledge that is then expanded on is a function of Jane's role as a governess, after all. However, another interpretation could be that this excess of information, coupled with the stilted nature of the sentences, could perhaps reveal that Jane's role as a governess is that of someone accustomed to keeping quiet, and so, when she does speak, her sentences lack order and appear haphazard.

Contextually, students could be encouraged here to discuss the lonely, isolated position of a governess within a household in the nineteenth century; neither lady nor servant, they often spent much time alone and would have had nobody of their status or intelligence to speak with on a day-to-day basis. As Jane is narrating the novel from the perspective of the adult looking back at her childhood, it can be argued that the first-person narrative frees the tongue that has always to be kept in check, explaining the almost frenetic nature of Jane's sentence construction. Jane's intelligence in her command of the English language – initiating her memory with a short, intriguing main clause that gives us no information before building a lengthy, complex sentence that provides additional description of the circumstance – also reveals her education in being aware of literary techniques and suggests an element of self-awareness. Jane is very consciously telling a story – her story – and she wants it to intrigue the reader. She very much wants her long-silenced voice to be heard.

At Key Stage 4, giving students a longer passage to analyse can be fruitful in enabling them to draw out patterns of sentence structure and how this is used to think about differences between characters. The construction of sentences delivered by the narrative voice is also worthy of analysis in many Key Stage 4 texts, with Jane Austen's use of free, indirect discourse being of particular interest. What should be taken further at Key Stage 4 is how sentence structure can reveal theme and context as well as character. In this extract from *Jane Eyre*, discussions around the themes of women's place in society and loneliness can be drawn out when thinking about why Jane might be using such long and complex sentences, ensuring that students meet all assessment objectives.

Key Stage 5: *A Streetcar Named Desire* by Tennessee Williams

Extract from Act One, Scene One

BLANCHE: I, I, I took the blows in my face and my body! All of those deaths! The long parade to the graveyard! Father, mother! Margaret, that dreadful way! So big with it, it couldn't be put in a coffin! But had to be burned like rubbish! You just came home in time for the funerals, Stella. And funerals are pretty compared to deaths. Funerals are quiet, but deaths—not always. Sometimes their breathing is hoarse, and sometimes it rattles, and sometimes they even cry out to you, "Don't let me go!" Even the old, sometimes, say, "Don't let me go." As if you were able to stop them! But funerals are quiet, with pretty flowers. And, oh, what gorgeous boxes they pack them away in! Unless you were there at the bed when they cried out, "Hold me!" you'd never suspect there was the struggle for breath and bleeding. You didn't dream, but I saw! Saw! Saw! And now you sit there telling me with your eyes that I let the place go! How in hell do you think all that sickness and dying was paid for? Death is expensive, Miss Stella! And old Cousin Jessie's right after Margaret's, hers! Why, the Grim Reaper had put up his tent on our doorstep! . . . Stella. Belle Reve was his headquarters! Honey—that's how it slipped through my fingers! Which of them left us a fortune? Which of them left a cent of insurance even? Only poor Jessie—one hundred to pay for her coffin. That was all, Stella! And I with my pitiful salary at the school. Yes, accuse me! Sit there and stare at me, thinking I let the place go! I let the place go? Where were you! In bed with your—Polack!

(London: Penguin, 2009, p.12)

WHY NOT CONSIDER?

- How does the use of exclamatory sentences reflect Blanche's personality?
- What is the significance of Blanche's interrogative sentences in showing the relationship between the sisters?
- How could the sentence structures in this extract function as a foreshadowing device?

In this speech of Blanche DuBois to her sister Stella in the first scene of the play, she reveals the loss of the sisters' childhood home, Belle Reve. However, the content of this speech also begins to reveal the extent of Blanche's neurotic personality in the way she expresses the experience to Stella. There is much to be said here about the type of language Blanche uses, but a sentence-level analysis can still offer much to students who will need to be able to discuss the structure of the text as well as the words Williams uses. There are a considerable amount of exclamatory sentences in this speech, demonstrating both Blanche's excitability and her dramatic take on events. Her use of exclamatory sentences shows a need to be the centre of attention, to make a scene; Blanche is casting herself as the actress in her own play here, and this self absorption and need to create a sense of dramatic significance in the telling of her experience is very revealing of her personality. Students can be encouraged to discuss how this sentence structure is a form of foreshadowing, hinting at how Blanche will slowly lose her mind later in the play as she blurs the lines between reality and performance.

The succession of short, simple sentences, many of them beginning with conjunctions, is also an interesting point for discussion. Blanche deliberately speaks with simple sentences, when in many cases she could have formed compound ones; this is evidenced in the fact that a large number of sentences begin with the conjunction 'and'. Her inability to form longer sentences could point to a disordered mind, one that is unable to stay on one topic for more than a short time. The succession of short, exclamatory sentences therefore builds a picture of a frenetic, over-wrought woman, and her occasional interspersing of these with interrogatives that do not require answers is of further interest, as she does not pause to allow these to be answered. These interrogatives are rhetorical, accusatory: part of Blanche's desire to blame her sister for her own failures, of course, but they could also be read as Blanche having a form of conversation with herself. She does not require an answer from Stella because she is answering her own questions with her exclamatory responses, which furthers the impression of Blanche's mental instability. Students could use this speech as a useful point of comparison with Blanche's later ones, where she really is talking to herself.

At Key Stage 5, students should be able to use grammatical constructions to make insightful comments about characters. This can often be most fruitful when looking at play scripts, but sentence-level analysis also works well in novels and poetry when thinking about how authors construct the voice of characters. More confident students can start to think about how character is shown through speech and what different sentence constructions can tell us about a character; students should be encouraged to see a character's speech as a deliberate extension of their personality. Try to avoid allowing students to make simplistic comments, such as simple sentences might suggest a lack of education or shyness; these are valid comments, of course, but this is the level of analysis that can be expected at Key Stage 4. Students studying at Key Stage 5 need to be thinking more critically about why characters' sentences are constructed in the way they are; what do they reveal about their personalities and the way they view themselves and others?

a better vessel to express this sentence's main idea. Rather than a long and quite unwieldy sentence, where the images become lost amidst an excess of unnecessary words, now the image of the golden carpet of leaves sings out and creates a more sophisticated and powerful image.

On a practical level, teaching grammar in this way can be really good fun as students can get competitively involved in the challenge of taking an initial group of sentences and working together to see how many different ways they can change the sentence and word order for effect. Students can vote on which rewrite they find most effective, and by playing around with different potential constructions they can be made aware of the huge array of choices available to them when constructing a sentence.

Another interesting challenge for students is giving them a section of published text and asking them to improve on it. Encourage your students not to see published work as sacrosanct: just because something is published doesn't mean it is perfect. Giving them the permission to play around with choices published authors have made to create different effects can also help them with their literary analysis skills, as they should be able to see more clearly, by changing sentences and seeing how that alters effect and meaning, why authors wrote the originals in the way they did.

Slow writing, where students write an initial piece of work on every other line of a piece of paper and then go back with a different coloured pen and rewrite it underneath, is a fantastic opportunity to enable them to think through their sentence choices. By taking the time to intentionally restructure their work, focusing on what they want their sentences to highlight rather than just thinking about how complicated they can make their writing, will, slowly but surely, lead to more thoughtful and successful writers.

SUGGESTED KEY STAGE 3 LESSON PLAN

Equipment needed:
Photocopies of paragraphs

L/O: To experiment with sentence structure in creating character

Starter (5–10 minutes)

Split students into small groups of three or four and give them two versions of the same short paragraph of dialogue, with each paragraph using slightly different sentence constructions (resource provided below). Ask students to read each paragraph carefully and think about the way they feel towards the characters after reading each one. Though the words the characters use remain the same, do they have the same response to the characters across the paragraphs? Encourage them to

Consider this rewrite:

Shivering, Isobel waited by the window. Shadows flitted through the freezing fog outside.

Reducing those two longer sentences to two much shorter ones creates exactly the same image, but the shortened length considerably increases the tension and sense of mystery. We now don't know why Isobel is waiting, but the short sentences create an atmosphere of anxiety and urgency. By beginning the first sentence with a verb followed by a comma, the sentence starts actively rather than passively and involves the reader immediately in the events. By separating the sentence into two clauses with the use of the comma after shivering, the idea of Isobel shivering is emphasised, leaving this image of her shaking with cold as the predominant one of the sentence, rather than it getting lost within the lengthy description in the first example. Likewise, by reducing the following sentence to a short, simple one, and beginning it with the word 'shadows', the emphasis is brought back to the element of mystery, making shadows the focus of the sentence rather than letting the word get lost amidst the unnecessary detail of the complex sentence in the first example. Helping students to understand how sentence construction and word order within sentences can be manipulated to emphasise the key parts of a story's message is vital to enabling more sophisticated creative writing. Merely encouraging children to write complex sentences wherever possible does not lead to more effective pieces of work, and students need to be trained to identify the key element of a sentence and how to construct the sentence to bring that element to the fore.

Example 2:

The trees in the garden were covered in golden autumn leaves that were slowly falling onto the ground below, creating a beautiful shining carpet.

Here a student wants to create an image of a colourful autumn scene, and they have used a nice example of imagery in the carpet to do so. However, this complex sentence structure is not allowing their image to sing out as it should do. The essential image of the sentence is lost as a subordinate clause, and needs to be brought out through changing the construction.

Consider this rewrite:

A shining golden carpet spread itself beneath the shivering boughs of the trees.

By reducing the complex construction to a simple sentence, and taking the content of what was previously a subordinate clause and making it the subject of a main clause, the image of the carpet becomes the predominant idea. Though the sentence is less complicated and doesn't use any punctuation, which some students may consider to be less effective, the reality is that the simple sentence construction is declarative or interrogative simple sentence that furthers his insistence that he is correct. Each sentence then has a third part, either another simple declarative or a simple interrogative, finally emphasising as part of this tripartite sentence structure that he will not listen to Emma's reason. This use of an either literal or implied, through the use of punctuation, tripartite sentence structure could be interpreted as a deliberate use of persuasive, rhetorical speech – the power of three – on Mr Woodhouse's part. By structuring his sentences in this way he could be said to be attempting to manipulate Emma's thought processes, taking an interpretation of his character to a more sinister level and providing students with a key feature of debate around whether Mr Woodhouse is really as benign as he seems.

Incorporating grammatical knowledge into creative writing

At Key Stage 3, where creative writing is a more dominant element of the curriculum, grammar can be used to help students make more deliberate, effective choices in structuring their writing. While most students at Key Stage 3 will be confident in using a range of sentence types in their work, articulating why a particular structure works more effectively than another, and making a more discerning choice about which type of sentence to use to create a particular effect, can be more problematic.

Writing well creatively should always start with being able to identify good examples of creative writing. The more students are able to analyse literature and understand the decisions writers make when choosing linguistic and structural features, the better they will be able to make thoughtful choices when putting their own words onto paper. Actively encouraging students to be critical writers as well as critical readers, assessing their own and their peers' work with an eye for detail and an ear for sound, enables them to edit their writing meaningfully, beyond just replacing words for more ambitious synonyms.

Example 1:

> *It was a cold night, and Isobel was sitting by the window shivering as she waited for her mother to come home. It was foggy outside, and the people who passed in the street were merely shadows as they flitted by.*

This piece of student's work is very good. The sentences are of complex construction and there are plenty of interesting adjectives. The use of fogs and shadows creates an intriguing atmosphere, with the reader able to conjure up an image of a cold and misty winter's night without much effort. However, to create a more powerful sense of mystery the sentence structures here could be altered considerably. Students often seem to think that the more complex the sentences they use the better the marks they will get, but this is a misunderstanding that needs to be corrected to ensure students can manipulate structure more effectively to build atmosphere within a piece.

Emma by Jane Austen

Extract from Chapter One

"Poor Miss Taylor!—I wish she were here again. What a pity it is that Mr Weston ever thought of her!"

"I cannot agree with you, papa; you know I cannot. Mr Weston is such a good-humoured, pleasant, excellent man, that he thoroughly deserves a good wife;—and you would not have had Miss Taylor live with us for ever, and bear all my odd humours, when she might have a house of her own?"

"A house of her own!—But where is the advantage of a house of her own? This is three times as large.—And you have never any odd humours, my dear."

"How often we shall be going to see them, and they coming to see us!—We shall be always meeting! We must begin; we must go and pay wedding visit very soon."

"My dear, how am I to get so far? Randalls is such a distance. I could not walk half so far."

"No, papa, nobody thought of your walking. We must go in the carriage, to be sure."

"The carriage! But James will not like to put the horses to for such a little way;—and where are the poor horses to be while we are paying our visit?"

(Ware: Wordsworth Classics, 2007, p.3–4)

WHY NOT CONSIDER?

- How does the contrast in the types of sentences used reflect the relationship between Emma and her father?
- What might the structure of Mr Woodhouse's sentences reveal about his character?

Above is another example to demonstrate more clearly how students can be challenged through the study of grammar at Key Stage 5. A simplistic analysis of the sentence structures in this extract would focus on how much Emma says compared to her father and then lead into a discussion of the power relationship between them, where Emma is like the reasoning parent and her father the querulous child. Emma's more adult vocabulary and complex sentence structure compared to the simple, exclamatory sentences used by her father show clearly how the generational difference between them has been reversed. This is all very straightforward and should not present much of a challenge for students at this level. However, pushing the sentence structure further here can lead to a more interesting analysis. The structure of the sentences arguably reveals Mr Woodhouse's selfishness. He begins each of his comments with a simple exclamatory sentence or an interrogative sentence, countering one of Emma's statements, before following this with either a look at the sentence structures and ask whether they have perhaps had a differing response due to this, leading them to refresh their knowledge of how different types of sentences can create different effects.

Main activity (35 minutes)

Move students into a position of working on their own, and ask them to choose a scenario and two to three characters for a short paragraph involving dialogue. The challenge in this activity will be for the students to build character, not through describing them but by allowing their personalities to shine through the sentences they use. They cannot use anything other than dialogue – no 'he shouted' or 'she screamed' etc. This will force them to think about interrogative, declarative and exclamatory sentences, and whether they want to show intelligence, thought, urgency etc. through the construction of simple, complex or compound sentences. Give students about 25 minutes to free write before allowing them to swap their work with a partner. The partners should write a summary of what they feel about the characters' personalities at the bottom of their peers' work, and then the students can discuss whether their partners were accurate in their assessment of the characters they created. Did purely using sentence construction work in allowing them to fully flesh out a character?

Plenary (15 minutes)

Allow students some time to share their own or their partners' paragraphs out loud and foster a whole-class discussion into their findings after this experience. What have they learned and how can they take this understanding further?

Differentation

For the main activity, if students are struggling to come up with ideas, provide them with a list of options, such as a mother and daughter arguing over whether the daughter can go out that night, friends complaining about another friend etc. For those students who need more challenge, add complexity by asking them to juggle three or four characters instead of just two. This activity could also be done in pairs for those students who find it hard to write by themselves.

Resource

Paragraph 1:

"You're never going to guess what I've just heard."
 "What?"
 "I'm telling you, you'll never guess."
 "Just tell me, Hannah."
 "OK. Listen. Remember yesterday, after school, when we heard that person crying in the toilets."

"Yes."
"Well. Apparently it was Sam Taylor, in 8A."
"And?"
"Priya told me it was because she got dumped by Jack for Nina."
"No way."
"It's the truth, I'm telling you. So anyway, he told Sam that she was boring and he was going out with Nina now."
"Ugh. I bet it's only because Nina won those tickets for the Bruno Mars concert and he wants to go."
"Probably."
"I never liked Jack anyway. Sam should never have gone out with him in the first place."
"Well, Priya says it's not even that Sam's upset about Jack. Apparently the main reason she's upset is because Nina said she'd take her to the Bruno Mars concert. And now she's giving the extra ticket to Jack."

Paragraph 2:

"You're never going to guess what I've just heard!"
"What?!"
"I'm telling you, you'll never guess!"
"Just tell me, Hannah!"
"OK, listen – remember yesterday, after school, when we heard that person crying in the toilets?"
"Yes."
"Well, apparently it was Sam Taylor, in 8A."
"And?"
"Priya told me it was because she got dumped by Jack for Nina!"
"No way!"
"It's the truth, I'm telling you! So anyway, he told Sam that she was boring and he was going out with Nina now."
"Ugh! I bet it's only because Nina won those tickets for the Bruno Mars concert and he wants to go."
"Probably."
"I never liked Jack anyway; Sam should never have gone out with him in the first place."
"Well, Priya says it's not even that Sam's upset about Jack! Apparently the main reason she's upset is because Nina said she'd take her to the Bruno Mars concert and now she's giving the ticket to Jack!"

 **Additional ideas**

Using sentence types to decode unseen texts

When first looking at an unseen text, a helpful way to start decoding levels of meaning can be through looking at the sentence construction before even beginning to look at the words being used. This can work equally well for non-fiction and fiction texts, as well as prose and verse texts. For unseen texts, looking at the number of complex, compound and simple sentences, as well as the use of exclamatory, interrogative or declarative sentences, can reveal much about the purpose and intended audience of the text. Are there plenty of interrogative sentences, designed to get the reader thinking? Or are there many declarative, complex sentences, suggesting it is designed for a more academic, serious audience? The same process can be gone through for fiction texts, by thinking about how characters' speech is constructed and what that reveals about them, as well as looking at poetry construction and thinking about how the types of sentence structures used reveal the mind of the poem's speaker.

As sentence types are so easy to identify and don't require any specialist knowledge in the way more complex grammatical concepts do (identifying specific types of verbs or nouns, for example), this is a fantastic way to ease your students into an in-depth textual analysis and have them come up with some interesting points without them feeling overwhelmed. It can also help students' confidence ahead of exam situations where they will be faced with unseen texts; knowing they have some simple decoding tools, such as looking at sentence structure to help them even if they don't fully understand the language or message within the text, can give much-needed reassurance.

Playwriting to encourage more thoughtful sentence construction

A way to encourage students to focus on deliberate, effective sentence construction is to get them to write short plays; as they will not be able to use any descriptive vocabulary to explain how their characters say their lines, they will be forced to focus on using sentence construction alone as a way to build character.

Summing up

Sentence structure can often seem unimportant compared to other, more complex, elements of a text that can be analysed or used for effect, but we hope this chapter has shown you how sentence structure can be a great way into more advanced analysis and creative writing skills. Far from being merely a basic structural form that needs little thought, sentence structure is something that allows character to be revealed and atmosphere to be created, and a sophisticated understanding of how sentences can be manipulated for effect can add much to students' appreciation of how texts are constructed. For those who are less confident with English, identifying sentence types is a fantastic way to softly introduce textual analysis as the rules are so easy to grasp. For students who are also less confident creative writers, manipulating sentence structures can feel far more manageable than the pressure of having to come up with ambitious vocabulary or figurative language choices. We hope you'll have fun experimenting with sentences in your classrooms and that your students will enjoy having their eyes opened to the many possibilities of sentence construction!

2 Nouns

Nouns are usually known as naming words, and they name people, places and things. A simple way to test if a word is a noun is to try putting 'the' in front of it (for example, 'dog' would work: 'the dog') or posing the question 'Do you know about...?' and inserting your word at the end (for example, 'courage': do you know about courage?). Not all nouns will fit into these structures but it can be a useful place to begin.

Under the umbrella of nouns are a number of other divisions.

Common nouns

Common nouns are used to classify things or to name general items rather than specific ones. For example:

Lorry, cat, lamp, grass and *table* are all common nouns.

All of these examples make sense if 'the' is put in front of them, and they can be added to the end of the sentence 'Do you know about...?'

These words explain what an item is and they don't require a capital letter unless they are at the start of a sentence.

Proper nouns

Proper nouns refer to something or someone specific, unlike the general referral in a common noun. They would usually have a capital letter at the start of the word and do not often use a determiner like 'a', 'an' or 'the' (although this is not always the case). For example:

London, Henry, Rolls-Royce, India and *Shakespeare.*

Concrete nouns

A concrete noun refers to something physical and tangible that can be held, touched, seen or in some way felt through the five senses. For example:

Violin, cup, smoke, country and *curtain.*

Abstract nouns

Abstract nouns refer to things that cannot be experienced through the five physical senses and refer to ideas, thoughts, time, emotions and qualities. For example:

Democracy, fear, month, joy and *courage.*

Noun phrases

A noun phrase includes a noun, either concrete or abstract, common noun or proper noun and the modifiers that tell us who it is in relation to something else, where it is, what it is doing etc. Of course, the type of modifiers used will depend on the context of the sentence. For example:

*The house **that is opposite mine**.*
*The girl **whose brother is in my class at school**.*

Count nouns

A count noun can have a plural form and therefore can be counted. To check if a noun is a count noun, see if it can be used after the determiner 'much'. If it can it is not a count noun. For example, using the count noun 'dog':

One dog, two dogs. Correct.
Much dogs. Incorrect.

Non-count nouns

Contrastingly, non-count nouns are qualities or attributes that cannot be counted and generally do not have a plural form. Unlike count nouns, the determiner 'much' can be used with them while the determination 'a' makes no sense. For example, using the non-count noun 'wealth':

One wealth, two wealth. Incorrect.
Much wealthier. Correct.

Some rare nouns can be both count and non-count nouns; for example, the word 'fish' can be used as both.

Pronouns

A pronoun is used in the place of a noun, noun phrase or noun clause. It is used when the noun has already been mentioned or is already known and is often employed to avoid repeating the noun. For example:

*Jane was hungry so **she** ate some toast.*
*Andrew took the dog with **him**.*

*Peter's leg was close to **mine**.*
***Anything** might happen.*
***That** isn't sensible.*

Pronouns can be broken down into a number of more specific groups, depending on their function and role within a sentence.

Personal pronouns

Personal pronouns are used in place of nouns and refer to specific things or people. First person personal pronouns are *I, me* (singular), *we* and *us* (plural) and they refer to the person or people who are narrating, speaking or writing. Second person personal pronouns are *you* (both singular and plural) and refer to the person or people being spoken or written about, as do third person personal pronouns. These are *she, he, her, him, it* (singular), *they* and *them* (plural).

These are broken down further into more specific categories:

Subject pronouns

Subject pronouns are used when the person or object being referred to is the subject of the verb. For example:

***She** kissed Sam.*
***We** walked to Robin's house.*
***I** waved at Roshona.*

Object pronouns

Object pronouns are used for the noun that is being affected by the action of the verb. For example:

*Can you help **me**?*
*I can smell **you**.*
*She doesn't like **him**.*
*I saw **her** in school today.*

Reflexive pronouns

Reflexive pronouns are used when the subject and the object in the sentence are the same person and will end in *self* or *selves*. Although that sounds complicated, they are used very frequently and often to create emphasis. For example:

*I saw **myself** as a complete failure.*
*She was worrying **herself** unnecessarily.*
*You should treat **yourselves** to an ice-cream.*

Singular reflexive pronouns are *myself, yourself, himself, herself* and *itself*, while the plurals are *ourselves, yourselves* and *themselves*.

Possessive pronouns

Possessive pronouns are used to show ownership or possession. For example:

*The horse is **mine**.*
*I believe that is **ours**.*
*The last table is **theirs**.*

The full list of singular possessive pronouns are *mine, yours, his* and *hers*, while *ours, yours* and *theirs* are the plurals.

Demonstrative pronouns

Demonstrative pronouns are used to show the relationship between the person speaking or writing and a person or a thing. The four demonstrative pronouns are *this, these, that* and *those*. The first two would indicate objects that are near to the speaker or writer, while the latter two refer to something or someone that is distant. For example:

*I like **these**, suggests something close by.*
*I like **those**, gives the impression of something far away.*

Interrogative pronouns

Interrogative pronouns, also occasionally known as question pronouns, are used for questioning. These are *who, what, which, whom* and *whose*. For example:

***Who** left the cup there?*
*To **whom** did you speak?*
***Which** belongs to you?*

Relative pronouns

A relative pronoun always directly follows the noun that it describes and often introduces a relative clause in the sentence. There are only five relative pronouns – *that, which, who, whom* and *whose*. For example:

*The dog **who** is barking lives next door.*
*I saw a horse **which** was escaping from a field.*

Indefinite pronouns

An indefinite pronoun doesn't refer to any specific person, thing or amount and is always vague. *All, another, any, anybody, anyone, anything, each, everybody, everyone, everything, few, many, nobody, none, one, several, some, somebody* and *someone* are examples of indefinite pronouns.

Putting it into practice

Now we have covered the different forms and categories of nouns that will be found in texts, we will explore how analysis of them will create a deeper understanding of the authorial intentions in literature. This has been split by Key Stage and also includes a section on creative writing.

Key Stage 3: *The Boy in the Striped Pyjamas* by John Boyne

Extract from Chapter Ten

Bruno slowed down when he saw the dot that became a speck that became a blob that became a figure that became a boy. Although there was a fence separating them, he knew that you could never be too careful with strangers and it was always best to approach them with caution. So he continued to walk, and before long they were facing each other.

"Hello," said Bruno.

"Hello," said the boy.

The boy was smaller than Bruno and was sitting on the ground with a forlorn expression. He wore the same striped pyjamas that all the other people on that side of the fence wore, and a striped cloth cap on his head. He wasn't wearing any shoes or socks and his feet were rather dirty. On his arm he wore an armband with a star on it.

(Oxford: David Fickling Books, 2006, p.106)

Thinking about nouns when looking at *The Boy in the Striped Pyjamas* can offer a great deal to discuss about status and characters' attitudes towards it. On many levels the novel is straightforward in its portrayal of injustice and discrimination, and few readers can fail to be moved and distressed by the subject matter. However, helping students to articulate how the writer helps them to feel the way they do, beyond the actual plot and characters, will support them in using language analysis to justify their responses to texts. Before starting a grammatical-level analysis, consider what you want students to draw out from the text. A guided approach is best with Key Stage 3 so that they can clearly link their grammatical knowledge to their interpretation.

> **WHY NOT CONSIDER?**
>
> - What is significant about the various common nouns used to describe the boy?
> - Could there be any value in exploring the fact that the boy is described using common nouns? What could you get out of exploring the notion of a 'common' noun being used to describe a unique person?
> - What significance could there be in the fact that there are many nouns in this extract but few adjectives?

This extract is significant as it is the first instance of Bruno meeting Shmuel. Students can be encouraged to use this extract from the novel as a key moment in their understanding of how difference and discrimination are shown in the text, and looking at the usage of nouns offers a perfect opportunity to enable students to articulate and justify these ideas. The litany of common nouns used to describe Shmuel – 'a dot', 'a speck', 'a blob' and 'a figure' – are all words that are never used to describe Bruno, who always has a keen sense of his own identity and his place within the world. These common nouns, all of which describe something unformed, insignificant and non-specific, reflect the treatment of the Jewish people, who are not considered human by the characters in the novel. The fact that Shmuel is described using common nouns also offers an opportunity for students to consider the meaning of the word 'common', as opposed to special or important, and whether the use of these types of nouns is deliberate on the part of the writer to emphasise how Shmuel is treated in comparison to Bruno, and how it reflects what those in power think of the Jewish people.

Another aspect of the extract students could look at is the use of 'the boy' as opposed to the proper noun 'Bruno', which depersonalises Shmuel and again reduces him to an insignificant, unremarkable person who doesn't have a name or identity of his own. The fact that he wears 'the same striped pyjamas', with the use of the determiner 'the', shows that these are not 'a' pair of pyjamas, unique to him, but a familiar, common type of pyjama that everyone in the camp wears, further removing any sense of Shmuel as the individual he was before he was brought into 'Out-With'.

The text as a whole uses simplistic language, and this extract highlights the lack of adjectives used by the author through its abundance of nouns. Very few of the nouns have a description, and this simplicity could reflect Bruno's simplistic viewpoint of the world. His lack of understanding of what is happening around him is key to the novel's plot, as it is Bruno's innocence that prevents him from seeing the reality of the cruelty and barbarism in which his father is wilfully participating. The uncomplicated prose, through its heavy use of nouns over adjectives, is something students could use productively as a way into exploring the ideas of innocence and appearance versus reality that are so important to an understanding of the novel's central messages.

Key Stage 4: *The Strange Case of Dr Jekyll and Mr Hyde* by Robert Louis Stevenson

Extract from Chapter Eight

"Ay, ay," said the lawyer. "My fears incline to the same point. Evil, I fear, founded—evil was sure to come—of that connection. Ay truly, I believe you; I believe poor Harry is killed; and I believe his murderer (for what purpose, God alone can tell) is still lurking in his victim's room. Well, let our name be vengeance. Call Bradshaw."

The footman came at the summons, very white and nervous.

"Put yourself together, Bradshaw," said the lawyer. "This suspense, I know, is telling upon all of you; but it is now our intention to make an end of it. Poole, here, and I are going to force our way into the cabinet. If all is well, my shoulders are broad enough to bear the blame. Meanwhile, lest anything should really be amiss, or any malefactor seek to escape by the back, you and the boy must go round the corner with a pair of good sticks and take your post at the laboratory door. We give you ten minutes, to get to your stations."

(New York: Signet Classics, 2012, p.94–95)

WHY NOT CONSIDER?

- Are concrete or abstract nouns the most dominant here? And how does this fit into what we know about the plot of the novel so far?
- How are pronouns used here and what does their use reveal about the characters?
- There is a distinct lack of proper nouns during this extract when Utterson, the lawyer, is being written about. What could this be suggesting?

If we start off by looking at the extract in the context of the novel as a whole, we can see immediately that Stevenson explores ideas about duality and how well anyone can really know another person, or even how well they know themselves. There's a lot of exploration of quite nebulous concepts, which by their very nature have abstract nouns attached to them, such as 'evil' and 'identity'. We find it is worth reminding students of themes like these before embarking on too much detailed analysis of an extract so that they have a frame to hang their ideas around.

If the nouns in the opening of this extract are listed as being either concrete or abstract, it becomes very interesting to note that, in a scene so concerned with the logistics of a situation, the abstract seems to dominate so readily. In the first full sentence spoken by Utterson we have 'fears', 'evil' and 'connection'. If we look at these we can see that Stevenson is using ideas about the lack of something tangible to help create fear. Ideas are so much more frightening for both an individual and society if they can't be definitively defined, and the unspoken and ambiguous use of 'fear' and 'evil', rather than an articulated common noun stating what might have happened, reinforces the idea that what has occurred is so awful it has been rendered unspeakable. As Utterson continues to speak, the use of concrete nouns such as 'murderer' and 'victim' only ramps up the mystery. Obviously, in the case of this novel, we do have to encourage those we are teaching to suspend their disbelief (every person in the classroom *knows* that the body that looks like Mr Hyde is the same man as Dr Jekyll, and have known from before they opened the book's first page) and view the mystery in Dr Jekyll's laboratory from the point of view of the clueless Utterson. These concrete nouns are common and not proper nouns – no-one can place an identity on either of these individuals, and so the mystery deepens.

This section clearly appears at a climactic moment in the novel, and so it is interesting that Utterson himself has changed from being referred to using a proper noun to the far less personal common noun. In fact, if we look through the text, we have the introduction by name of Bradshaw, the footman, while Poole, the butler, keeps his proper noun nomenclature, but twice in quick succession Utterson is now 'the lawyer'. It seems that Stevenson is making a suggestion that, as the action advances, Utterson is no longer there as a personal friend of Dr Jekyll but has instead become the dominant figure in control of events that have floored Dr Jekyll's servants, and this is demonstrated with his professional title. Poole and Bradshaw are humanised by the proper nouns, reinforcing the idea that the events in the laboratory are greatly affecting all the individuals in the house, while providing a contrast with Utterson – now 'the lawyer' – who through his status as a professional, and an outsider, shows that, however respectable one is, it is never possible to completely know them. Utterson himself reinforces the rigid social hierarchy of the time through his use of common nouns, casually referring to a very junior member of the household as 'the boy', as though his lowly employment status removes the need for him to be recognised as an individual, and declaring that he, Utterson, as a member of the ruling classes, has 'shoulders . . . broad enough to bear the blame' if needed. Although he uses the common noun 'shoulders', there is clearly a metaphorical use of the word, suggesting again the responsibility that a professional man at the time would assume, while the abstract noun 'blame' again hints to us of the reticence to really speak of anything unpleasant in a specific way.

It might be useful for students to go through the extract, again bearing in mind the mood of ambiguity and suspense that Stevenson has created with this balance of abstract and common nouns, and then look at how the emphasis and ambiguity is shifted when these two are substituted for the other.

Key Stage 5: *Wuthering Heights* by Emily Brontë

Extract from Chapter Four

We crowded round, and over Miss Cathy's head I had a peep at a dirty, ragged, black-haired child; big enough both to walk and talk: indeed, its face looked older than Catherine's; yet when it was set on its feet, it only stared round, and repeated over and over again some gibberish that nobody could understand. I was frightened, and Mrs Earnshaw was ready to fling it out of doors: she did fly up, asking how he could fashion to bring that gipsy brat into the house, when they had their own bairns to feed and fend for? What he meant to do with it, and whether he were mad? The master tried to explain the matter; but he was really half dead with fatigue, and all that I could make out, amongst her scolding, was a tale of his seeing it starving, and houseless, and as good as dumb, in the streets of Liverpool, where he picked it up and inquired for its owner. Not a soul knew to whom it belonged, he said; and his money and time being both limited, he thought it better to take it home with him at once, than run into vain expenses there: because he was determined he would not leave it as he found it. Well, the conclusion was, that my mistress grumbled herself calm; and Mr Earnshaw told me to wash it, and give it clean things, and let it sleep with the children.

(London: Oxford University Press, 1957, p.42–43)

This extract is significant as it describes Heathcliff's arrival and offers an intriguing glimpse into his childhood treatment at the hands of various members of the Earnshaw family. A more psychological reading of the text can find plenty of material here to explore how and why Heathcliff becomes the man he does, but the key to a successful analysis is in rooting the response firmly within Brontë's linguistic choices.

> **WHY NOT CONSIDER?**
>
> - What is the significance of the use of pronouns in this extract?
> - How does the use of 'it' objectify Heathcliff and how could this be tied into a discussion of his origins when considering the Liverpudlian context?
> - How could this passage stimulate conversation about the psychological impact on Heathcliff of hearing himself spoken about in this way when he is in the room?

This should not be a difficult extract for Key Stage 5 students as the quite obvious use of the pronoun 'it' to describe Heathcliff, rather than 'he' or a name, completely depersonalises and objectifies him, marking him out as an 'other' and as something unidentifiable, inhuman and unwelcome. This can feed into a discussion of Heathcliff as an animalistic or possibly supernatural creature; the fact that he is not even given a gender by Mrs Earnshaw shows how abnormal he is viewed as being by the other characters.

More subtle ways of looking at the use of pronouns here can lead into very fruitful discussions about the nature of Heathcliff's origins. The fact that he is objectified as an 'it' and is referred to as having an 'owner', as well as having been found in Liverpool, could offer an intriguing interpretation of Heathcliff's background. Perhaps the depersonalising pronouns are being used because Heathcliff was a slave, or related to a slave, and so, in the eyes of his contemporary society, is less than human. Liverpool was a key trading port in the slave trade in the late eighteenth and early nineteenth centuries, and the fact that Heathcliff is described as 'dark' and like a 'gipsy' clearly suggests he looks something other than Caucasian in appearance. As such, this objectification through the use of pronouns could have been a deliberate device by Brontë to point to Heathcliff's possible slave origins, which would also explain the exaggerated horror of Mrs Earnshaw when she sees him.

This passage and its use of impersonal pronouns could also provide a springboard for discussion about Heathcliff and how much of his behaviour in adult life can be traced back to his childhood. The fact that he was referred to as 'it' by his adoptive parents could arguably have caused significant psychological damage, and this objectifying of Heathcliff and insistence on his insignificance could conceivably account for the violent way he behaves towards others. Rather than merely making vague psychological inferences about Heathcliff's past in order to justify this type of interpretation, students can use grammatical constructions such as these pronouns to ground their analysis firmly within the text and provide a sophisticated linguistic basis for their ideas.

 ## Creative writing

Often at Key Stage 3, students can see nouns as something immovable: an object needs a 'handle' and there is only one option. A boat is always just a boat, and, although it can be dressed up with adjectives or similes, the noun is a constant that they can't seem to change. But for more adventurous writers, exploration of their noun choices can actually be an inventive way to stretch themselves to produce far more ambitious and imaginative writing.

Consider the use of visual or auditory prompts so that students can write a description in their usual way, without immediately focusing on nouns, so that, when an improvement is made, students are able to appreciate how much difference this new approach makes. By asking them to compare their work and use of nouns with that of *The Boy in the Striped Pyjamas* or any other text you've been studying together, they should quickly see the point being made about the significance of replacing proper nouns with common nouns, and how important the implicit message behind those choices is. Because of this approach (basing noun analysis largely on character for Key Stage 3), creative writing should also be character-based. This is an opportunity to enlarge or improve on a character already existing in a narrative they are creating, or could be a chance to use a minor character from a novel or a play as the basis for a description and the exploration of the importance of nouns.

The creation of word banks through starter activities can be a helpful support for students who struggle with this type of activity, especially as many students can find it hard at first to consider that common nouns *can* be replaced in their work. For example, starting with a common noun such as 'boat' there are obvious synonyms or alternatives, such as 'ship', 'vessel', 'sea-craft' or 'dinghy', and most students will feel happy to brainstorm these. However, differentiation can occur when you push students to move beyond the literal and see the noun as an opportunity for a metaphor. Suddenly the boat is no longer just 'a life-raft' or 'a punt', but it could be an abstract noun such as 'safety' or 'a watery prison'. By making certain nouns 'taboo' during writing exercises, students will have to expand the way they use their vocabulary and consider an abstract noun that suggests the same idea or hunt for a replacement through metaphor.

The modelling of suggestions is always helpful during creative writing, and sentence starters and suggestions are particularly appreciated by students who have more limited vocabularies, such as those for whom English is an additional language. Nouns can be especially challenging if there is the need to find a more complex or unusual synonym. However, by challenging students to think of a metaphor or comparison, so that the common noun is replaced by a symbol or an unexpected abstract noun, this can be the chance for more confident students to shine. Even using a highly prized object, such as the latest must-have mobile phone, can get students thinking about what the alternative is to the literal common noun. Is it abstract, like success or kudos, or is it a metaphor, like an emperor's crown or a rapper's sports car? Framing nouns in creative writing in these terms can be a very useful starting point.

SUGGESTED KEY STAGE 3 LESSON PLAN

This lesson plan uses Witch Child *by Celia Rees (Bloomsbury, 2009) as the basis, but can easily be adapted to any novel or text suitable for Key Stage 3.*

Equipment needed
Copies of the text
Coloured pens or pencils
List of common, concrete nouns for plenary

L/O: To analyse character through nouns

Starter (5–10 minutes)

In groups or pairs, students need to list all the significant characters that appear in *Witch Child* and any description that accompanies them; so, for example, Jaybird's grandfather describes Mary as being like a 'young she wolf' (p.166) because she is 'fierce, proud and brave but not fully grown into her strength'. Martha is seen by Mary to be 'past her middle years' (p.34) with her hair 'streaked with grey, and her skin wrinkled as a winter apple but her eyes were bright and sharp'.

Ideas can then be shared in a larger class discussion, or with 'ambassadors' from each table exchanging information. These ideas will form the basis for the lesson's main creative writing task, so it is worth ensuring that everyone has a good breadth of characters and an idea of how Rees has described them.

As there's been a chance for some creative writing, now is the time to move onto a quick recap about what a noun is, and the difference between common and proper, and abstract and concrete nouns. Ask students to look at the descriptions they have and consider which nouns are being used most and how they are being used.

> **STARTER ACTIVITY PROMPT QUESTIONS:**
> - Does Rees use more common or proper nouns?
> - What sort of imagery does she favour? Are nouns appearing in similes, metaphors or personification?
> - Which do you find most effective?

Main activity (35 minutes)

Students can either pick a character they have covered in the starter activity or can be allocated one. Beginning with the description they have already, the nouns are now the focus point. If Rees has used the common noun of 'she wolf', what can they replace this with to evoke the same idea of the character or to deepen the reader's understanding of it? Moving beyond just finding a synonym replacement, they should try to incorporate ideas for proper, abstract and concrete nouns, all building up a more complex and interesting idea of the character.

Features such as eyes, hair or hands should be subject to a 'taboo' – students cannot use these common nouns but have to find an alternative to suggest these features. The aim is for students to think about what they can suggest through the use of metaphor; making a direct comparison and saying that Mary has, for example, 'two penetrating glittering stones that can perceive far beyond what normal people discern', instead of talking about eyes, or that Jaybird walks on 'soles that are as sensitive as a newly hatched bird', to avoid mentioning his feet.

After enough time has been given for ample descriptions to be produced, tell students to swap their work. They now need to identify the noun choices in the description and label them. Often this can interrupt the flow of the lesson, so it could be worth providing coloured pens for underlining and having a key on the board so that everyone knows a red line means a proper noun, a yellow line denotes a common noun, and so on. Once these have been identified they are then a fresh pair of eyes to the character sketch and it is the students' job to make improvements. As students approach Key Stage 4, the ability to draft and then redraft is important, particularly in creative writing, and this activity supports this skill using an incremental step – it is often far easier to improve someone else's work if you don't feel emotionally connected to it, rather than to be neutrally critical of your own work. In this case, if they see a lot of concrete nouns, the challenge is to change these to abstract nouns, and to see if they can evoke a sense of what these represent through less tangible ideas. If proper nouns are dominating, how can these be changed to common nouns while evoking the same sense?

Work should then be returned so that a final redraft is possible, and then ideas can be shared either through class discussion or in pairs or small groups. It can be satisfying for students to compare their original work with the improved piece so they can see how far they have come.

Plenary (5–10 minutes)

The plenary is for consolidating the idea that picking obvious common nouns in descriptive writing can be too predictable to produce a really arresting character description, so this quick-fire activity is designed to ensure students get used to thinking beyond the usual to something far more inventive. Common, concrete nouns will be displayed at random (you can do this easily by simply scrolling through words on a PowerPoint presentation or even look up how to create a word generator on Excel) and, in teams, students will be challenged to come up with as many synonyms for the word as they can, with bonus points given for any metaphor replacing the noun entirely, or abstract noun which suggests something it might represent. So, for example, if the word 'spectacles' is displayed, students might suggest 'glasses', 'pince-nez', 'sunglasses' or 'face furniture', but could also have 'intelligence', 'insight' or 'vulnerability', or a metaphor such as 'fragile instruments of perception'. Aim to cover at least five nouns and share answers at the end. If you're feeling generous you could award a prize of a concrete noun such as sweets, or the use of praise if you're feeling more abstract!

Differentiation

Those who need more support might find that being given a list of descriptions of the characters and a list of character names, with the challenge being to match the two together, is a more manageable start to the lesson. During the main task some students might struggle to analyse the work of others, so it might be worth preparing some short examples for them to look at (with post-it note labels of the different noun classes so they can stick them on the examples) that are tailored to the correct level of challenge. When changing the nouns, tables might wish to centrally work on one character sketch to increase their confidence, or to have a word bank of alternative suggestions which they can rotate in and out of the text to see which works best.

Stretching and challenging more able students can begin at the start of the lesson when they can be tasked with imagining peripheral characters which could exist outside of the narrated action, such as some of the villagers who persecuted Mary's grandmother at the start of the novel or some of the villagers who left Beulah after disagreements with the village authorities. Coming up with a brief character sketch for them, using the same style as Rees' writing, is a great way to challenge able writers to think carefully about language choices.

The list of 'taboo' nouns could be increased during a challenge to spot clichés. Which comparisons and metaphors do students feel appear too regularly or are too obvious? By asking high-performing students to spot these and then consciously ignore them, their vocabulary becomes more ambitious and a higher level of sophistication appears in their writing.

SUGGESTED LESSON PLAN FOR KEY STAGE 4 ANALYSIS

This lesson plan is designed to be adaptable for any fiction text, hence we do not refer to any text in particular.

Equipment needed
Post-it notes
Pens
Copies of text

L/O: To analyse character through use of abstract nouns

> **AS A QUICK INTRODUCTION TO THE LESSON, WHY NOT TRY:**
>
> - Asking students to come up with an abstract noun they feel summarises the novel.
> - Asking students to choose an abstract noun to describe their favourite character from the novel.
> - Asking students to choose an abstract noun that they definitely wouldn't choose to describe the novel/a favourite character.

Starter (10 minutes)

Often when analysing character the focus is on adjectives, with students using them to discuss characters' appearance and personality. Looking at the abstract nouns used to describe a character and banning students from considering adjectives can therefore be an interesting and challenging way to explore a character from a slightly different perspective. We would start the lesson on abstract noun analysis by asking students to choose a key character on whom they want to focus their analysis. Students can then be challenged to think of nouns that are used to describe the character in the text and write them down. Depending on whether this is a lesson towards the beginning or end of studying the text, or a revision task, you can decide whether you allow students to use their books to prompt them or challenge them to rely on their memories. Making this a memory task can be especially effective if students have been working on memorising quotations for an upcoming exam. Once the students have been working for about seven minutes, allow them to find someone else who has also chosen their character so they can compare and contrast responses. Any additional nouns they can pick up from their partner should be added to their list.

Main activity (40 minutes)

Task 1 (10 minutes): Students now take their list of nouns and pick out the five that they feel are most worthy of further exploration when it comes to analysing their character. Ask students to write each of these down on a post-it note and add all the words they can think of associated with that noun. These nouns could be to do with personality, profession, status, intellect – allow students to be free with their interpretation of what is significant about that character. For example, if a student chooses the noun 'innocent', then they may choose to write associative words such as 'childlike', 'victim', 'weak', 'powerless', 'injustice', 'naïve' etc., of course depending on the context of the novel they are studying. If students are struggling with this it may help to do an example together on the board before starting, or make it a pair-work task.

Task 2 (15 minutes): Once everyone has finished with their post-it notes, ask the students to form groups of three or four and to take their post-it notes with them. They are not to tell their group members which character they have analysed. Together they will look at the post-it notes they have all completed and sort them into character piles, deciding which character they feel each post-it note best represents. Students must argue out their differences to come to a consensus – there can be no post-it note left without a character assigned to it. Groups should then feed back to the rest of the class about their findings, discussing any insights they have gained through looking at the noun-association words on the various post-it notes they have explored in their group. Encourage them to discuss any interpretations they didn't agree with, as this can often lead to very fruitful debate! An alternative way of conducting this activity is to do it as a whole class. You could collect the post-it notes from the students, stick them on the board and then ask students to come up and sort the notes into the correct characters before discussing them together. This would work particularly well in a small class setting or as a revision activity.

Task 3 (15 minutes): Students should now have a good understanding of a range of noun-based interpretations of the various characters in the novel. Ask them to choose their favourite noun analysis of their character that they have come across during the lesson – this may be the analysis they did or an analysis by a classmate – and write a short, analytical paragraph, using quotations, to explain the significance of this noun to the interpretation of their character's role within the novel. If time is short this activity could be an oral one, with students taking it in turns to explain in three sentences their favourite noun interpretation and why they thought it was so successful. For more challenge, or for something a little different, you could also ask students to do the opposite; which interpretation did they think was least effective and why?

Plenary (10 minutes)

Students should now pair up and peer assess each other's paragraphs, giving constructive feedback on the quality of their response. How much has the noun analysis helped them to deconstruct the character and their significance within the text? Once the students have swapped back, if there is time, allow some students to share their work, picking out and elaborating on any particularly pertinent points that shed a more unusual/subtle insight into a character. Alternatively, if time is short, conduct a quick oral round robin of each student's favourite noun and why it could work well here to round off the lesson and assess the quality of the learning.

Differentiation

Support students who need a little more guidance by providing them with a pre-prepared noun list for each character, with some associative words already given to help them get started on their analysis. Those who need more challenge could be given some antonyms for nouns used to describe the characters in the book and asked to suggest what they think the original noun is. They could also argue why the antonymic nouns are not effective at describing the character and what alternative nouns could be used instead.

An additional challenge activity, or an alternative starter for a more revision-focused lesson, could be to give students a prominent section of text where a key character is described with the nouns blanked out. Students would have to try to fill in the blanks with appropriate nouns to test their knowledge of the text.

Additional ideas

Use of nouns when analysing unseen poetry

Nouns should be seen as a safe haven for students during unseen poetry, as they're easy to spot and likely to be vocabulary that they're familiar with. However, in spite of this there is still often a sea of anguished faces when students are asked to look at this element in an unseen poem. By honing their approach, hopefully this element will be easier for them to access and allow them to distil the poet's message more easily.

Looking first at the nouns used, students can discern whether or not a particular type of noun is dominating. Is there a listing of objects suggesting a narrative voice that is trying to create control or hang on to memories? Are there lots of abstract nouns denoting a poem about ephemeral ideas, fears or intangible worries? Are nouns being repeated for emphasis? By breaking down the nouns like this, students can start to access the meaning of a poem.

You can also encourage students to consider how some common nouns have other connotations, particularly when they are looking at texts for GCSE. You can prompt them to consider the importance of historical and social context in this respect. For example, the frenzied repeated mention of the noun 'hair' in poems such as Robert Browning's 'Porphyria's Lover' and Charlotte Mew's 'The Farmer's Bride' shows the fetishising of revealed body parts of females in the nineteenth century, and students can start to pick up clues about narratives and characters. It is also worth students thinking about the sounds that nouns are making, especially as these appear so frequently. Are they considering a fricative or sibilance element to nouns which they encounter? What is the impact on the tone of the poem from this?

Analysis of nouns can often provide great insights into the mood, tone or topic of the poem, and by considering these ideas students have a hook on which to start to hang their ideas. With careful analysis of this element, students can begin to approach unseen poems with a positive attitude and with some of the fear taken away.

Use of nouns when studying Shakespeare

When teaching Shakespeare at all ages, nouns can be a fantastic and fun way to access tricky passages of text.

Let's first look at *A Midsummer Night's Dream*. A popular Key Stage 3 text, this is often students' first exposure to Shakespeare. The central scene, Act 3 Scene 2, can be reduced and made into a funny, and very brief, sketch if students work in small groups to perform the roles of Helena, Hermia, Lysander and Demetrius – using nouns only. They will quickly understand the key ideas of the scene and note the number of aggressive names the characters call each other! This idea can be used with any Shakespeare text at any age. Reducing scenes down to the most essential nouns tackles students' fears of not being able to understand the text by removing any confusing adjectives or complex sentence constructions, allowing them to clearly identify the key points that Shakespeare wanted the audience to understand. With classes that are reluctant to perform, such as recalcitrant sixth formers, getting students to pull out the key nouns and write them on pieces of paper before shouting them at each other in unison can be a fun way to achieve the same effect without students having to feel exposed in front of the class.

An interesting way to explore *Macbeth* and the key early scenes between Lady Macbeth and Macbeth, when Lady Macbeth is persuading her husband to kill Duncan, is to look at the use of pronouns. Asking students to pair up and play the roles of Lady Macbeth and Macbeth, pointing either to themselves or to the other every time the character uses a pronoun (i.e. if the character says 'thou', they need to point at their partner; if the character says 'my', they need to point to themselves), can help them to see who is dominant in the scene and who is thinking more about themselves, opening up character interpretation and ideas about motivation.

At all levels, pulling out nouns used to refer to a character and placing them on post-it notes to play any number of interpretative games can be useful for active starters, plenaries or quick-fire revision. Students can use noun post-its to help them develop character analysis, identify characters, identify which character calls others particular names, identify thematic patterns within the text etc. Noun post-its can be used as a starting point for quote prompting ('which quote includes "the stars"?'), as a character identification game ('who calls who a "canker-blossom"?') or as a vocabulary builder ('what does "hurly" mean?'), along with many other matching and identifying games that you can encourage students to devise for themselves and their classmates.

Noun washing lines can also be a useful activity for revision while doubling up as attractive classroom decoration! Put up string, get some mini clothes pegs, and then ask students to write key nouns for each character on colour-coded paper, each character having a different colour assigned to them. Peg up the paper on the string line and then watch students miraculously quote Shakespearean nouns in their work before long! This idea can obviously also be used for any other texts being studied in class to aid with quotation memorisation.

Summing up

Nouns are a key component of literary analysis, yet they can be so easily overlooked or simply lumped together as the hook for an adjective to be attached to. Hopefully this chapter will have allowed you to examine how fundamental they are in exploring character and theme. We can judge a lot about authorial intentions when we look at the use of common, rather than proper, nouns attached to characters, while the exploration of themes is made easier if we start to look at the significance of either concrete or abstract nouns within the text. Armed with this knowledge you'll feel confident to explore a huge range of ideas with your students based around nouns, and, as a result, your insights into texts will be greater and lessons should be easier to plan and more interesting to teach.

3 Verbs

Verbs are the basic building blocks of language, telling us what someone or something is doing or what is happening. All children in Key Stage 3 and above should easily be able to identify verbs in sentences, and, certainly for native speakers, conjugating verbs within a sentence of any tense should not pose too much of a problem. However, many children – and teachers! – may struggle to identify which exact form of verb they are using and why, or the name of the verb tense and what that tense signifies. A solid understanding of different tense constructions and the different functions of a verb within a sentence can enable students to make a more precise analysis of a character or writer's intention, as well as help the students to construct more effective sentences in their own writing. For those working in an environment where there are a number of EAL students, it will also be of significant help to your students if you are able to explain clearly the exact uses of tense constructions to avoid grammatical mistakes and confusion between simple, continuous and perfect tenses.

Verbs can be split into different categories depending on their role within a sentence, and conjugated into different tenses. We'll look at the different categories first and then the tenses.

The infinitive

The infinitive is the verb in its purest form and is usually preceded by 'to'. The infinitive is the basis for all conjugation into various tenses and derivatives. For example:

*Amir decided **to eat** all of his sister's chocolates as well as his own.*

Here, 'to eat' is the verb in its infinitive form; there is no need to change it in order to have the sentence make sense, as the verb 'to decide' has already been conjugated into the past simple tense earlier in the sentence (decided), indicating who did the action and when the action took place.

The main verb

This can also be referred to as the **principal verb**. Many sentences contain more than one verb, and in order to differentiate between them a verb can be described as a 'main' or an 'auxiliary' verb. A main verb is the most important verb in the sentence, telling us the **action or state of being of a subject**.

It is important that students understand that main verbs are not always actions, as this is often where people can become confused. In the sentences *'my mother is a lawyer'* and *'there are some grapes in the fridge'*, the 'is' and 'are' are the main verbs, even though they are not describing physical actions taking place.

If we once again use the example of Amir above, in this sentence 'to eat' is an infinitive and so not the main verb. 'Decided' is the main verb, because it is telling us the action. The main action of the sentence is not the fact that Amir is eating the chocolates – it is that he has **made a decision** to eat the chocolates. The sentence doesn't actually tell us whether Amir has eaten the chocolates or not at this point in time – but we do know that Amir has made a decision, so that is the main verb of the sentence.

Auxiliary verbs

Auxiliary verbs are, simply put, 'helping' verbs. They help form different tenses, moods and voices. The main auxiliary verbs are to be, to do and to have.

To be is used to form continuous tenses and the passive voice.
Present continuous tense: *I was running late.*
Passive voice: *The piano was played by Tom.*

To have is used to form **perfect tenses**.
Past perfect tense: *She had been told not to come.*
Future perfect tense: *We will have more of those in stock on Tuesday.*

To do is used in several different ways.
First, for emphasis: *I did do my homework, I promise!*
Second, to form questions: *Do you have a minute to talk?*
Third, to form negative phrases or questions: *Don't speak to me like that! Don't you think you should have thought about that earlier?*

Modal verbs

These are a form of auxiliary verbs and they express necessity, possibility, intention or ability. These can also be known as conditionals, as they are verbs describing actions and states of being that are conditional on other events.

The modal verbs are: must, shall, will, should, would, ought (to), can, could, may and might. Modal verbs are particularly useful when starting to teach students how to write literary essays. Reminding students of modal verbs to help them express ambiguity enables them to add sophistication and maturity to their analytical writing.

Transitive and intransitive verbs

A transitive verb is one that is used with an object. An object can be a noun, phrase or pronoun, depending on the sentence, but no matter what form it takes, the object will always be directly affected by the action the verb is describing. We sometimes remind students to think of a transit van, an object, to remind them that the transitive form needs an object. For example:

She wrote a story.

Here, *wrote* is the transitive verb and the *story* is the direct object.

An **intransitive verb** does not have an object. For example:

They ran in the park.

Here, *ran* is intransitive because no one is affected by the action of running.

Many verbs can function as both transitive and intransitive verbs, depending on the content of the sentence. For example:

Sarah is painting.

Here, the *is painting* functions as an **intransitive verb** – Sarah is not painting anything in particular so there is nothing to be affected by her action.

However, in the sentence *Sarah is painting a beautiful picture*, the *is painting* becomes a **transitive** verb because there is something affected by her actions – the beautiful picture.

Active and passive

The active and passive voices are essential constructions for students to understand, particularly when studying non-fiction texts. In a sentence, verbs can either be active or passive, depending on the wording and who is performing the action.

The simplest way to explain the difference is that in an active sentence the subject is performing the action, and in a passive sentence the action is done to the subject, or the subject receives the action. A trick we teach our students is that if you could add 'by zombies' to the end of the sentence then it's in the passive voice (i.e. 'I went shopping' couldn't have 'by zombies' added, therefore it is active. However, 'my shopping was bought for me by zombies' makes perfect sense, and therefore it is clear the sentence is passive).

The passive voice is formed by using the relevant conjugation of the verb 'to be' and the past participle of the main verb.

Example of a present simple passive (am/are/is + past participle): *He is always given a lift to work by his friend.*

Example of present continuous passive (am/are/is being + past continuous): *They are being followed by a stray dog.*
Example of present perfect passive (have/has been + past participle): *The company has been bought by overseas investors.*
Example of past simple passive (was/were + past participle): *They were instructed not to walk on the grass.*
Example of past continuous passive (was/were being + past participle): *Jake's trainers were being ruined by his sister.*
Example of past perfect passive (had been + past participle): *They had been seen behind the curtains.*
Example of future passive (will be + past participle): *They will be taken to another place.*
Example of future perfect passive (will have been + past participle): *Nothing will have been finished by tomorrow.*

Reflexive verbs

A reflexive is a verb whose direct object is the same as the subject. Put simply, the person or object performing the action is performing it on or against or to themselves. Reflexive verbs are always transitive as the reflexive pronoun 'self' is being affected by the verb. For example:

> She **washed herself**.
> The party was so good that they all **enjoyed themselves**.

Phrasal verbs

A phrasal verb is a verb coupled with an adverb, preposition or both together to form a phrase. Often these phrases have a metaphorical rather than literal meaning and can confuse non-native speakers of English. For example:

> I'll **see to it** that she doesn't come to my party.
> If you can, **put** him **off** until Tuesday.
> He **broke up** with me.
> She couldn't **keep up with** the other runners.
> They wouldn't **back down** on their original offer.

Phrasal verbs can be transitive or intransitive. As can be seen in the example of 'put him off', phrasal verbs can be separated by the insertion of pronouns or nouns if they are transitive. If they are intransitive they cannot be separated. For example:

> *He was put off his lunch.* (transitive)
> *His lunch put him off.* (intransitive)

Moods

A mood in grammar relates to the way in which thought is being expressed. A verb can take on five potential moods, depending on what is being communicated.

These moods are:

Indicative (statements of fact): *I am coming right now!*
Imperative (commands and instructions – always uses the infinitive without 'to'): *Keep off the grass!*
Interrogative (to ask questions – always uses an auxiliary with the verb): *When is she coming?*
Conditional (to make requests or express uncertainty – uses might/would/should with the verb in the infinitive form, though with no use of 'to'): *Could I have some coffee, please?*
Subjunctive (to express wishes or possibilities – uses third person present singular conjugation of the verb): *If I were a fantastic swimmer I'd compete in the Olympics.*

Verb tenses

Tenses tell us when someone or something performed an action, or when something existed or happened. There are three main tenses:

Present tense (present simple)

This is the most commonly used tense, used to describe what is currently happening or what always happens. *(It is raining. I am shopping.)*

Past tense (past simple)

This tense is used to describe things that happened before the present time of speaking. This can be a one-off event or something that happened repeatedly. *(I ate dinner. She looked sad.)*

Future tense (future simple)

This tense is used to describe things that haven't yet happened but which are expected or likely to take place in the future. The future tense is always formed with will or shall. *(I will see her tomorrow. They will arrive at seven.)*

Each of these tenses has its simple form as detailed above, as well as **continuous and perfect forms.**

The perfective aspect

The perfective aspect denotes viewing the event the verb describes as a completed whole, rather than something which is happening or did happen. So, for example, *she knelt down* as opposed to *she was kneeling down*. Since the focus is on the completion of the action expressed by the verb, it is usually used in the past and future tenses rather than the present.

The continuous aspect

The progressive aspect expresses an on-going action and will have the suffix *-ing*. It is used to show an action that will be continuing for a long time or something new, temporary or changing, and can be in the past, present or future tense. Examples include:

Continuous forms, also known as progressive, express actions that continue over a period of time and don't have a clear start or end point. They are formed by the relevant tense of the auxiliary *to be*, and the **present participle** of the main verb.
the **present continuous** (*I am writing.*)
the **past continuous** (*I was writing.*)
the **future continuous** (*I will be writing.*)
Perfect tenses are used to express actions that are either completed at the time of talking or were or will be finished by a particular point in the past or future. They are formed by the relevant tense of the auxiliary verb 'to have' and the past participle of the main verb.
the **present perfect** (*I have written.*)
the **past perfect** (*I had written.*)
the **future perfect** (*I will have written.*)

Perfect continuous

The perfect continuous, as suggested by its name, is a combination of perfect and continuous tenses. These are formed and used as follows:

the **present perfect continuous** (*I have been writing*): used to talk about how long something has continued up until now.
the **past perfect continuous** (*I had been writing*): used to talk about something which continued up to a particular moment in the past but is now completed.
the **future perfect continuous** (*I will have been writing*): used to talk about something which is expected to end by a particular time in the future.
the **past progressive tense** (*He was writing*): used to talk about continuing action that happened in the past. The tense is formed with the 'to be' verb, in the past tense, plus the present participle of the verb (with an *-ing* ending).
the **present progressive tense** (*I am writing*): used to talk about an action that is going on now and is continuing. Again, the verb 'to be' is used, along with the present participle of the verb, also with the *-ing* ending.

the **future progressive tense** (*I will be writing*): used to talk about a continuing action that will be taking place at some time in the future. Rather than simply combining with 'to be', as in the past progressive and the future progressive, this is formed with the modal 'will' and then 'be' plus the present participle of the verb with the *-ing* ending.

Participles

Participles are words formed from verbs, usually by adding *-d*, *-ed* or *-ing* to the end, although there are a number of verbs that are irregular. Participles are either in the present or past tense.

The present participle always ends in **-ing**.

The past participle ends in **-d** or **-ed** for *regular* verbs and usually **-en** or **-t** for *irregular* verbs, although there are some that don't follow this pattern and are the same as the infinitive (such as become) or have a different ending entirely (such as forgone). As past participles can be problematic, students should be encouraged to learn the more unusual ones to prevent mistakes; this is particularly relevant for EAL students.

Participles are used with auxiliary verbs to make verb tenses, as we have seen above with perfect and continuous tenses. They are also used to form the **passive tense** (*we were told*), as **adjectives** (*she sat on the broken chair*) and **nouns** (*the doctor told him to stop smoking*). When a present participle is used as a noun it is also known as a **gerund**.

Participles therefore play an important role in sentence construction and can perform many different functions.

Putting it into practice

Now that we have covered the different forms and categories of verbs that will be found in texts, we will look at how analysis of these supports an understanding of writers' intentions in literature, as well as informing better creative writing choices. We have split our examples by Key Stage to enable you to see a variety of texts and levels of analysis.

 Key Stage 3: *The Graveyard Book* by Neil Gaiman

Extract from Chapter One

There was a hand in the darkness, and it held a knife. The knife had a handle of polished black bone, and a blade finer and sharper than any razor. If it sliced you, you might not even know you had been cut, not immediately. The knife had done almost everything it was brought to that house to do, and both the blade and the handle were wet.

(London: Bloomsbury, 2008, p.3)

> **WHY NOT CONSIDER?**
>
> - How many different types of sentences are there and in what order do they appear? What significance might this have?
> - Is there a contrast between the active and passive voice? If so, what significance might this have?
> - How does the use of verbs contribute to the mood of the extract?

When analysing an extract from the perspective of seeing how verbs affect the meaning, we think it is most helpful to first identify the mood and tense before moving on to look at active and passive voice, transitive and intransitive construction etc.

Therefore, if we look at the tenses first, we can see what knowledge and understanding we can glean from the extract. The first sentence is past simple, as is the second. The third and fourth are a mixture of past simple and past perfect. The first two and fourth sentences are indicative in mood, reporting facts, and are in the active voice. The third sentence is a conditional, exploring what might happen if the knife were to cut you, and is in the passive voice. Already we can see a highly effective pattern developing here. The third sentence differs in its verb construction and so stands out from the ones around it. While they report the disturbing facts about the knife in the immediate, direct form of the active past simple, the third sentence is more complex in construction. Its conditional mood and passive voice invite us as readers to contemplate the future possibilities of what the knife might be capable of.

In the first two sentences we switch between the hand and the knife being the subject. Both are disembodied, active creatures that have a will of their own. This sense of a will of their own is heightened by the use of intransitive verbs; no one is directly affected by the actions of the knife in this early section of the text. We are not told what it has done as there is no named object, adding to the sense of mystery and suspense. The modal verb 'might' encourages the reader to consider, amidst this lack of information, what the knife could do; this modal verb construction creates an uncertainty that heightens the eerie quality of the scene.

All of these observations about the types and moods of verbs enable readers to be able to articulate how and why the opening section of the novel is so disturbing: it is clear that the opening section is disturbing, but being able to identify the reasons why on a grammatical level is much more challenging. Most students should be able to spot the fact that many of the verbs are negative, which is a fantastic start. However, a closer analysis using technical vocabulary and showing a clear understanding of grammatical constructions leads to a more meaningful and complex appraisal of the choices the author has made.

Key Stage 4: *Lord of the Flies* by William Golding

Extract from Chapter One

The boy with fair hair lowered himself down the last few feet of rock and began to pick his way toward the lagoon. Though he had taken off his school sweater and trailed it now from one hand, his grey shirt stuck to him and his hair was plastered to his forehead. All round him the long scar smashed into the jungle was a bath of heat.

(London: Penguin, 1964, p.7)

> **WHY NOT CONSIDER?**
>
> - How does the verb construction reveal Ralph's personality in this opening extract?
> - Is there a contrast between the active and passive voice? If so, what significance might this have?
> - What is the difference between the verb construction used to describe Ralph and those used to describe his surroundings? What significance might this have?

The verb choices Golding makes in the opening chapter of *Lord of the Flies* are helpful for us to consider, for, although they are subtle, they position Ralph as an individual caught between the civilisation of his previous existence and the wildness of the island where he now finds himself. We can immediately start looking at how the wider themes of the novel are reflected in these simple language choices, and at Key Stage 4 it is helpful for students who are now comfortable with terms such as transitive and intransitive, active and passive, to start thinking about how these terms illuminate the text.

The opening sentence is compound in its construction, where the first verb is straightforwardly in the past tense, with the reflexive, transitive verb 'lowered himself'. It is very clear, after reading the novel and during deeper analysis, that the use of the transitive verb highlights to us that 'the boy', Ralph, immediately has an impact on his surroundings through his actions, setting the tone throughout the novel of the boys disturbing the island and leaving a deep, and often destructive, impression. The reflexive 'himself' also demonstrates to us that Ralph is a character with purpose to his actions, as well as a strong sense of self-possession and control: this is likely to be significant later in the novel. It might be helpful for students to consider, if this opening were written with different verb choices – such as an intransitive verb, or in the first person, for instance, with a subjunctive – how this could alter our perceptions of this character.

The sense of purpose that surrounds Ralph is echoed immediately in the second sentence, where the quick succession of transitive verbs confirms Ralph as able to act decisively. This impression is solidified by the author's use of the active voice. Golding's verb choices are already setting Ralph up to be a leader; perceptive readers can glean much from these two seemingly straightforward sentences.

In sentence three, Ralph is no longer the subject of the verbs and attention moves on to his surroundings through the use of the past perfect tense. This firmly shifts the emphasis onto both the physical impact of the plane's landing (it had 'smashed into the jungle') and the stifling temperature (it 'was a bath of heat'). The past perfect tense of these verbs suggests that, thematically, the scar created by the smash is likely to be significant, with Golding pointing to the destructive elements of human nature and clearly foreshadowing the emotionally stifling and volatile nature of the island.

Moving away from the opening sentences, it is also worth considering how verbs illuminate our understanding of different characters. For instance, Jack begins the novel by mixing his use of more conciliatory modal verbs with imperatives, revealing his innate sense of command and autocratic tendencies as he barks 'Stand still!' and 'Sit down. Let him alone' within a matter of lines. Students can track his use of imperatives through the novel, until the climax and his final utterance of 'Heave! Heave! Heave!'

Dissecting Golding's use of modal verbs can also be useful in illuminating the differences in the characters of Ralph, Jack and Piggy. It is possible to see their character arcs developing – as well as gaining an insight into their personalities – simply by isolating these and considering the degree of modality in their choices. For example, Jack moves from his assertion in Chapter Two that 'We ought to have more rules', with use of the inclusive pronoun suggesting that creating more rules is a good idea, to poking another boy in the ribs and telling him 'You got to join my tribe' in the chapter Castle Rock. Ralph tends to use the positive 'can' while Piggy, with his repeated use of 'could' and 'should', shows he is weighed down with obligations he cannot hope to make the other boys follow.

 ## Key Stage 5: *Dracula* by Bram Stoker

Extract from Chapter Two

> *5 May—I must have been asleep, for certainly if I had been fully awake I must have noticed the approach of such a remarkable place. In the gloom the courtyard looked of considerable size, and as several dark ways led from it under great round arches, it perhaps seemed bigger than it really is. I have not yet been able to see it by daylight.*
>
> (London: Penguin, 2003, p.21)

> **WHY NOT CONSIDER?**
>
> - What is the significance of modal verbs in this extract?
> - How does the use of verbs explore the ideas of fear and uncertainty Stoker wishes to convey?
> - What effect do the varied tenses have?

At Key Stage 5, students can glean much from a close analysis of verbs in order to discuss with increased subtlety the motivations of both the characters and the author. *Dracula* is a popular Key Stage 5 text, with the focus usually on the supernatural or the Gothic, and so this analysis will look at how connections can be made between the language and the overarching themes. Jonathan Harker's description of his arrival at Dracula's castle begins with the use of modal verbs to construct the present perfect and the past subjunctive tenses. The use of these modal verbs to express uncertainty immediately emphasises the confused and bewildered state of Jonathan as he arrives at the castle. The castle causes him to feel unsure of himself; he cannot be certain whether he was asleep or awake. The modal construction adds to the Gothic sense of liminality between fantasy and reality that the castle introduces to the text. We move between the past and present perfect tenses in this extract, adding to the sense of uncertainty; Jonathan moves from describing what the castle looked like, in the past simple, to moving to the past perfect when saying 'I have not yet been able to see it by daylight'. His grammatical merging of the past and present reflects his disordered state of mind. The abrupt change between past and present emphasises the present tense sentence, making the reader realise with some alarm that Jonathan has been trapped inside the castle since his arrival and also hinting at the danger yet to come.

While this analysis of the uncertainty and foreboding in the opening passage is not new from a literary criticism perspective, what it offers is the technical vocabulary to enable students to describe in detail why there is such a sense of uncertainty and foreboding. It is all very well for students to say that the use of negative vocabulary such as 'gloom' and 'dark' and the uncertainty between waking and sleeping create a sense of the Gothic or supernatural, but the ability to articulate how this effect is created on a grammatical level allows them to provide more concrete reasons why readers feel the way they do about the text. It also allows students to move away from simplistic comments about the use of vocabulary and really demonstrate a solid understanding of how language is constructed, which is vital for examination success.

50 Verbs

 Creative writing

Key Stage 3

After becoming so familiar with the use of verbs, and what they can reveal in others' writing, students can then feel empowered to use verbs creatively and accurately in their own narrative and descriptive writing tasks. By understanding the implications of verb tense and type, they are more likely to be able to harness this knowledge when writing themselves.

Reinforcing the need for powerful and appropriate verbs is important for students at Key Stage 3, and a way to make them consider this in their creative writing is through description. Using a picture prompt as a starting point, supply your class with a written description of a painting – for example, *Impression, Sunrise* by Monet – and write the description without verbs. You could write:

'Muted colours in the sky, with smudges of dusky orange and grey. A boat and two tiny figures, the sea vast and mild. The sun round and recumbent in the sky, the mood tranquil and still. Muffled outlines of boats, vast and imposing.'

Ask your students what they think and what could be done to improve this passage, steering those who find this more of a struggle to recognise it has been written without the use of verbs. Challenge them then to attempt a description free of verbs and discuss the difficulties this creates. By acknowledging the limitations of descriptive writing *without* verbs, we are highlighting their importance to students. This will prompt them in a second draft, where they are free to explore and include language fully, to consciously use more exciting and vibrant vocabulary.

It can also be helpful to spend time redrafting with students, considering whether or not the verbs they have used are as imaginative and full of impact as possible. Again, by removing verbs from a description, leaving a blank where they should be, students can think for themselves what would be most appropriate. Looking back at *Impression, Sunrise* as an example, you could write:

With the soft circumference of the blurred sun _____ing in the sky, there is a soft and muffled sound as clouds are _____ing across the horizon. The tang of salt _____ the sailor's breath as his weary arms _____ the oar as the dusky sea _____. The smudged silhouette of the rigging _____ the landscape and _____ the tiny boats.

Paired work can also be undertaken, where students compare their choices and explain why they have chosen them. Using other colleagues' verb choices in their own descriptions, and noticing the differing effect this has, can be another way for students to explore the importance of verbs in creative writing for Key Stage 3.

Key Stage 4

The difference between active and passive verbs is straightforward, and nearly all students will have grasped it by Key Stage 4. As well as being useful for factual writing, such as in newspaper articles and reports, these verbs can be incredibly revealing about character when students use them in narrative writing. It is worth spending time exploring their differing implications.

To begin with, students could be presented with a narrative idea; for example, two young people camping in the woods. Depending on the ability or experience of the students, provide as much or as little detail as is needed. Some classes may only need to know that there are two young people in the wood and that they are camping. Others may be reassured to have a checklist of information such as:

- Two young people, both females, aged 17.
- They are away from home doing research in the woods for a school project on fungus.
- The story opens in the late evening, when they are preparing for bed.
- As the narrative progresses they are frightened by a noise in the trees, which one girl goes to investigate while the other stays at the tent to look after their belongings.

By asking the students to produce two different narratives, one written in the passive voice and one written in the active voice, it is a real opportunity to discuss how each is constructed (remember to share the zombie trick with anyone who is unsure) and which is the most appropriate when trying to build tension, elicit interest in the characters or create sympathy. For example:

> 'The torch was grabbed by Sunita and the light rapidly extinguished. The sound of breathing, jagged and indecently close, was heard by both girls as the tent door was rapidly yanked shut.'

> 'Sunita grabbed the torch and rapidly extinguished the light. Both girls heard the sound of breathing, jagged and indecently close, as they rapidly yanked the tent door shut.'

It is immediately clear to most students that the use of the passive voice frames Sunita and her friend as more victim-like than is the case with the active voice. It is worth exploring a number of narrative scenarios – such as someone committing a crime, or falling in love, or mistaking the identity of a person they are meeting – to discern whether active or passive is the best voice to create an intended effect.

Exploration of sentences featuring transitive and intransitive verbs is also useful at Key Stage 4, when the majority of students will be comfortable with the concepts and be able to recognise them in the work of others. However, their use as a tool may need to be reinforced before they are used creatively in narrative, and a quick reminder (transitive verbs are used with objects and the action has an effect, whereas an intransitive verb has no object) is often a useful starting point. For example, using the same scenario as above:

'*Sunita grabbed the torch*' (transitive because the torch has clearly been affected) and '*Sunita grabbed wildly in panic at the noise*' (intransitive because she doesn't actually grab anything or anyone).

As before, the important step is to move beyond just creating the narrative sequences to analysing what they reveal about a character or the plot and how this effect is achieved. In the first sentence we can see Sunita as a decisive character who is taking action to be in control of the situation, whereas the intransitive second sentence shows the character to be more vulnerable and far less able to act effectively in the face of threat.

SUGGESTED KEY STAGE 3 LESSON PLAN

Equipment needed
Picture as a stimulus for description
Teacher-written description without verbs
Teacher-written description with verbs blanked out (if appropriate)
Two thematically similar pictures or sounds for the plenary

L/O: To experiment with the use of verbs in creative writing

> **STIMULATING DISCUSSION**
>
> Get students thinking at the start of the lesson by asking whether verbs are necessary for creative writing. Is there a type of word we tend to use more than others when we try to be creative? This should stimulate some interesting discussions around what words students try to be more creative with: verbs are usually at the bottom of the list!

Starter (5–10 minutes)

With the image either displayed at the front of the classroom or waiting for students on their desks, the lesson should begin with a warm-up exercise of students brainstorming – either individually, in pairs or in small groups – the vocabulary that the image inspires them to think of. Results should be written down as useful prompts for later independent writing. Ideas can then be spread by 'ambassadors' from each table visiting other groups to share vocabulary and exchange ideas (or be more speedily shared through teacher-led feedback).

Main activity (40 minutes)

The verb-less description can now be shared with the class, and time given for either teacher-led or peer discussion. It might be helpful, if some students are struggling, to identify the limitations of the description by asking them to look back at their own brainstormed vocabulary list and reflect on which types of word dominate; it is likely that adjectives and nouns will have made up the majority of contributions. By nudging students in this way, and leading them with questions such as 'What is stopping this being a complete sentence?' or 'What sort of word would we expect to find with a noun and an adjective that we might now be seeing here?', many will see what is missing. This is a useful chance to pause and for students to examine their own vocabulary list, reflecting on why they see verbs as less helpful in descriptions than many other word classes. Some students may be inspired to add verb choices, especially infinitives, to their list.

With verbs now very much the focus, students can write their own descriptions of the scene, utilising either the word bank from the starter activity or supplementing the teacher's description with verbs so that each language fragment is turned into a complete sentence.

Depending on the length of the lesson (or the length of the description!) there could be an opportunity for students to learn from their peers. This is done by swapping work, spending time identifying the verbs in the descriptions and coming up with synonyms or improvements before moving on to cover verb tenses and their impact.

For this section of the lesson it is likely to be useful for some students if you either provide a written prompt or have a brief discussion of the verb tenses you are going to be writing in, and examples. Ensure that everyone is entirely clear on the terms you are using, perhaps by asking them to use a simple example, such as describe eating your breakfast in the present simple tense ('I am eating my breakfast') and then in the present progressive ('I have been eating my breakfast'). They should now rewrite their description in both tenses, and articulate which is most appropriate for the task. Support could be given for this more challenging task in the form of sentence starters, such as 'The present continuous gives an impression that the scene is melancholy because. . .' for students who are struggling to perceive the difference in meaning.

Repeating these steps for the perfective aspect ('I ate my breakfast') and the past continuous aspect ('I was eating my breakfast') can also be incredibly illuminating for students and gives them, with the verbs in different tenses, at least four examples of the same description. Time should then be given for them to reflect on which overall has been the most effective, and why. Students should then be encouraged to articulate this and think of other examples where different verb tenses might well be more appropriate in their creative writing.

Plenary (5–10 minutes)

The final minutes of the lesson are a crucial time to consolidate the idea that verb choices have a huge impact on the mood and atmosphere of a description, and the accuracy of what they display. Students should now be challenged to put these skills to the test by being given two thematically similar stimuli and, using only differing verbs, highlighting the variations. For example, in one picture the marl-grey sky *is starting to threaten* the earth, while in the other the marl-grey sky *is seeming to subdue* the earth. These examples should also be explored in the tenses that have been used in the main activity, to give insight into which tense is most appropriate to create certain atmospheres and impressions. Adequate time should be left to share some answers with the class, particularly to see if others can guess which description fits which image or sound purely from the choice of verbs.

Differentiation

Those who are less sure of word classes may need a prompt reminding them of verbs, nouns, adjectives, adverbs etc. so that they feel equipped to identify the missing words as verbs. Less confident students may also appreciate a word bank of verbs, with some more challenging pieces of vocabulary provided with definitions and modelled sentences containing the verbs. Some may also like the first blank space filled for them to model how the exercise works. Examples of the verb tenses, or a sheet with options to pick from, may assist those who struggle with this aspect.

More confident students could also be challenged to include more esoteric verb choices, such as an intransitive verb, a gerund or an ancillary verb. They could also be asked to change the verb tense (for example, from present simple to the continuous aspect) and then analyse what impact this has on the pace or the mood of the writing. For those who work quickly, the description with the verbs blanked out could be an opportunity to swap in different verbs which display high-level vocabulary and to then decide which most accurately reflect what is shown in the image.

SUGGESTED KEY STAGE 4 LESSON PLAN

Equipment needed
Short narrative for starter activity, written in the passive voice
Outline of a narrative (if required)
Fragment of narrative for the plenary, either teacher-written or from published work

L/O: To experiment with using the active and passive voice

Starter (5–10 minutes)

Although it might be tempting to begin the lesson with a straightforward recap of transitive and intransitive verbs, and the active and passive tense, this seems a slightly dry beginning to a session where creativity is so important. It would also put the emphasis firmly on the mechanics of how these verbs work, when the lesson needs to focus far more on the effect they have. Resist the temptation, and instead begin with this focus in mind: the lesson is about reinforcing the thought behind verb choices, and this is where to begin.

Give the students a short narrative opening written in the passive tense, and suggest to them that the focus of their analysis be on character. What can be deduced about the characters in the narrative? How are they being presented and why is this important when forming an opinion of them? Allow time for the students to reach their conclusions, perhaps in small groups or in partnered work, before bringing the class together in a wider discussion. Perceptive students may have already noticed the use of the passive voice, and guided verbal questioning could also be used to ensure everyone reaches this conclusion. Now is the time to make sure that there is certainty from students on what each voice is and how to recognise it. To ensure clarity on all four forms use examples, if needed, about the journey to school: 'Edward took the bus to school' is an active example; 'Edward was taken to school by bus' is passive; 'Edward walked to school' is intransitive; and 'Edward walked on the pavements to school' is transitive.

Main activity (40 minutes)

Using a suggested starting point for a narrative opening – for example, 'Write the opening of a story about an incident when weather was important' – gives students time to work on the beginning of the same story in both passive and active voices. Before they begin they must produce a brief character outline for the same character in each narrative, indicating how they will be portrayed in contrasting ways through the differing use of passive and active voices. Their protagonist in the active voice narrative could be strong, decisive and ready for action, while in the passive voice the character is faced with the same set of circumstances but, purely by switching the verb choices, will appear meek, helpless in the face of difficulties and highly susceptible to the influence of surrounding events. It is important to emphasise that the same events (some sort of crisis or event produced by extreme weather) will occur in both narratives and that noun choices are likely to be largely the same, so that the real way for the character differences to be perceived will be through the active and passive voices.

Students will gain a lot from reading the character sketches partners have done and then matching these descriptions to the contrasting narratives. After reading another's work or listening to a peer's example read aloud, it can be illuminating for students to consider what sort of character they have just heard or read about and to note down which specific verb choices have created this impression. Again, this should reinforce the central influence of the active versus the passive voice in portraying character in a narrative.

Moving on to transitive and intransitive verbs, students are now tasked with developing their narratives so that they are trying out the effect of changing transitive verbs to intransitive, and analysing how this changes the atmosphere or the emphasis of a piece. It might be helpful for this to be broken down into steps for some students, so that they first identify the verbs in question and only then change them. It is important that the lesson has adequate time for reflection, as more will be gained by students if they are given a chance to consider the effect of the verb changes rather than concentrating on simply identifying and changing the verbs. Group or class discussion can be a great way to bring clarity, especially if focusing on questions such as 'Which version makes the protagonist seem most in danger?' or 'Does the transitive verb or the intransitive verb build the most tension?' Students will then be able to not only use verbs effectively in their writing, but will also be able to recognise the impact the verbs are having in any writing they analyse.

Plenary (5–10 minutes)

As a way of consolidating the lesson's learning, the plenary looks at recognising the verb classes and their effect and then seeking to change them. Students will be given a small fragment of narrative and be tasked with identifying whether active or passive, transitive or intransitive, verbs have been used, and will note down the atmosphere of the writing and any impression they have of the characters. They will then quickly rewrite the fragment using the opposite voice and verbs. Working in pairs, students then swap the writing and decide what has been revealed about atmosphere and character before comparing how this differs to the impression created by the original narrative fragment.

Differentiation

As before, those who are less sure of the vocabulary might need reminders such as visual prompts detailing the difference between active and passive, and transitive and intransitive verbs. Less confident students may also appreciate a prompt to base their narrative on, or even some visual stimulation as a starting point. A word bank of suggested vocabulary for the characters in the narrative or to describe atmosphere could support struggling students. For those who find the task very hard, adapting a narrative with blank spaces and optional words might allow them to access the ideas about the different effects of the verbs without having to write anything themselves.

Higher-ability students can also be challenged in this lesson to change not just from active to passive, or from transitive to intransitive, but to consider tense at the same time. Does the use of the passive voice work differently in the present simple to the past tense? If the intransitive verb is moved from the past tense to the present continuous, what effect does this have?

Additional ideas

Use of verbs when analysing unseen poetry

Unseen poetry is often the element of an exam that instils most fear into students, despite their familiarity with poetic terms. A verb-based analysis of a poem can help students draw out meaning and make insightful analyses of a poet's intentions, helping them to feel their way into a poem and make sense of it before moving on to look at other aspects of language and structure.

Students can first identify the verbs and what mood and tone these create: can they all be grouped together as being the same mood and tone, or are there distinct groupings within the poem, perhaps marking a volta, change of circumstance/attitude, or sense of uncertainty? Students can then look at the tense or tenses used, and what this might reveal; for example, a present tense narrative voice might have a very different effect and purpose to a past tense.

Intransitive and transitive constructions can also provide worthy material for comment: if there is no object affected by the actions of the subject in a line, what could this reveal (and vice versa)?

Once students have completed a grammatical analysis of this nature they should be able to identify the tone, topic and effect of the poem to a considerable degree, giving them a confident basis from which to build further analysis. Starting with a verb-level approach will, hopefully, demystify and simplify the poem sufficiently to allow them to tackle an essay without feeling any fear!

Modal verbs in Shakespeare: extending students' understanding

Macbeth, Act 1 Scene 7, line 32

Macbeth
We will proceed no further in this business:
He hath honour'd me of late; and I have bought
Golden opinions from all sorts of people,
Which would be worn now in their newest gloss,
Not cast aside so soon.

Lady Macbeth
Was the hope drunk
Wherein you dress'd yourself? hath it slept since?
And wakes it now, to look so green and pale
At what it did so freely? From this time
Such I account thy love. Art thou afeard
To be the same in thine own act and valour
As thou art in desire? Wouldst thou have that

Which thou esteem'st the ornament of life,
And live a coward in thine own esteem,
Letting "I dare not" wait upon "I would",
Like the poor cat i' the adage?

(Oxford: Oxford University Press, 2009)

This extract, when Macbeth and Lady Macbeth are arguing over whether or not to murder Duncan, is often used to demonstrate Macbeth's uncertainty and his wife's more prominent role in persuading him to do the deed. A closer look at the extract, with a focus on modal verbs, offers an interesting analysis of their relationship and could be a challenging extension task for more able students at Key Stage 3.

First of all, Macbeth's use of the modal verb 'will', when saying 'we will proceed no further in this business', is definitive and clearly expresses his certainty of intention. The use of 'will' therefore suggests that he has decided he does not want to kill Duncan, and his mind is clear on the matter. However, his later use of 'would', when describing how he wants to rest on his laurels in benefiting from his new title for a while, demonstrates how it would be a little premature in declaring that this speech reveals Macbeth's decided frame of mind. The fact that he says 'which would be worn now' implies an 'if' – they would be worn now if he weren't to do something to prevent it – which shows he is still entertaining the concept, the possibility, of not being able to wear his new titles in their 'newest gloss' thanks to having murdered Duncan. In this light, the 'will' at the beginning could therefore be viewed as a form of bravura; Macbeth comes in to speak to Lady Macbeth all guns blazing, but his use of modal verbs reveals the fact that he is far from certain – either of his own mind or his ability to stand up to the response he already knows his wife will give.

Lady Macbeth's use of 'wouldst' in her speech has a far more deliberate purpose. She uses the modal verb to set up a contrast to goad Macbeth – would he want to live a coward in his own sight, or have what he really wants? Her use of 'would' allows her to project a negative image of the future onto the events, unsettling Macbeth from his pretence at certainty demonstrated in his previous speech. Lady Macbeth uses modals, therefore, as a persuasive device: very telling of her manipulative personality.

Analysed in this way, the modal verbs give a more subtle analysis of the Macbeths' personalities and the power struggle within their relationship. This discussion of modal verbs could also be coupled with sentence-level analysis of the use of imperatives to draw out how Shakespeare is using grammatical constructions in this exchange to reveal the Macbeths' troubled relationship.

Summing Up

Verbs can seem such a vital part of sentence construction that they are hardly worth our notice. We hope this chapter has shown how interesting a vehicle they can be in allowing greater insight into authorial intentions, while also adding sophistication and deliberate thought to creative writing. Verb tenses can reveal so much about a character's perceptions of themselves or of events, and manipulating verb tenses in their own writing can give students the ability to make subtle inferences about these. There is much more to verbs than meets the eye, and we hope you now feel comfortable in discussing them in more detail with your students.

4 Determiners

In simplest terms, determiners modify nouns. They can be both referring or quantifying, so telling us whom the noun belongs to, where it is, and how many of them there are. Determiners always come before a noun or noun phrase and are often ignored entirely as being insignificant. However, a good understanding of the types of determiners that exist and what they signify can add a great deal to students' analyses of literature.

Determiners can take several forms.

Referral determiners are:

Articles

Articles are *a/an* and *the*. 'A/an' is known as the indefinite article because it is not referring to anything specific, and 'the' is known as the definitive article because it is referring to something specific. For example:

> *I bought **an** ice-cream.* There is no specification of which type of ice-cream, so this is an indefinite article.

If we wanted to make the article definite we would need to change the sentence to:

> *I bought **the** ice-cream with sprinkles.* This time we need the definite article because we are referring to a specific type of ice-cream, as opposed to the many others available to us.

Possessives

Possessive determiners are *my, your/s, her/s, his, its, our/s* and *their*. Possessive determiners and pronouns are possible to tell apart in a sentence by looking at their role. Pronouns replace full noun phrases; possessive determiners come before the noun to tell us to whom it belongs. For example:

> *Don't touch that coat! It's **ours**!* Here 'ours' is a pronoun, because it replaces the noun entirely.

*She brought **her** coat.* Here 'her' is a possessive determiner because it describes the noun, telling us whom the noun belongs to.

Demonstratives

Demonstrative determiners are *this, that, these* and *those*. They allow us to explain which specific noun we are referring to and whether it is close to us (*this, these*) or further away (*that, those*). Like possessives, demonstratives can also be used as pronouns, and the difference can be seen when looking at the sentence structure: if the demonstrative is modifying the noun it is a determiner; if it is the subject of the sentence then it is a pronoun. For example:

This *is my coat.* Here 'this' is a pronoun and not a determiner because it is not modifying the noun and is the subject of the sentence.

This *coat is mine.* Here 'this' is modifying the noun 'coat' and so it functions as a determiner within the sentence.

Quantifying determiners are:

Quantifiers

Quantifiers tell us how much/many of something there is. Examples of quantifiers are *some, many, few, little, several, much, less, all, any*. The use of these varies as to whether they are being used with countable or non-countable nouns, or whether the amount is known or not known.

N.B. Numbers can also be classed as quantifiers.

> **WHAT ABOUT WHOSE AND WHICH?**
>
> These can be tricky to define. They are only determiners if used in the interrogative progressive form, before the noun:
>
> **Which** *shoes should I wear?*
> **Whose** *coat is this?*

Putting it into practice

Now we have covered the different forms and categories of determiners that will be found in texts we will explore how analysis of them will create a deeper understanding of authorial intentions in literature. This segment has been split by Key Stage and also includes a section on creative writing.

Determiners are everywhere, in all texts. While frequently there may not be an enormous amount to say about their role, being as they are such a necessary part of speech that many writers may not pay much attention to them from a creative perspective, there can still be much to consider about interpretations of determiner choices if students are vigilant and prepared to be imaginative.

 ## Key Stage 3: *Goodnight Mister Tom* by Michelle Magorian

Extract from Chapter 3

When Willie awoke it was still very dark. Straining his eyes, he could just make out the two boxes which were stacked in the far corner of the room and a picture frame which was propped against them. He raised his arms and touched the sloping ceiling above his head. The pain that had brought him sharply back to consciousness seared violently through his stomach. He held his breath and pushed his hand down to the bed to touch his night-gown. It was soaking. It was then that he became aware that he was lying in between sheets. That's what they did to people after they had died, they laid them out in a bed. He sat up quickly and hit his head on the eave. Crawling out of bed, doubled over with the pain in his gut he hobbled over to the window and let out a frightened cry.

(London: Puffin Books, 2011, p.37)

It is easy now we've looked at what determiners are to see their frequency in this extract. Analysis of them might seem a challenge for Key Stage 3, but if we think about what we are trying to encourage students to grasp about Willie's character and his reaction to the situation he finds himself in, then determiners can provide us with a way into the text which, although not obvious, can be illuminating.

> **WHY NOT CONSIDER?**
>
> - When is the author using a possessive determiner and when is there use of definite articles?
> - What does this tell us about Willie's preoccupations and the reaction he has to his surroundings?
> - Look at the frequency of indefinite articles versus definite articles. How does this colour our reactions to his surroundings?

The idea of analysing an extract through determiners might seem daunting for those in Key Stage 3, but, by considering first impressions of characters and the situations they are in, students can think about how this seemingly small element can support the conclusions they have drawn during their first reading. We instinctively know the importance of Willie's body, emphasised through his pain, and the disconnection he feels for his surroundings, but by looking at specific language choices we can show even the most nervous reader how they provide a way in to further textual understanding.

The obvious sensation we get from this short extract is that of Willie as a boy in lots of physical pain, and this is emphasised for the reader through the repeated use of a possessive determiner when talking about his physical self. The sense of Willie as a physical being who has endured abuse and so is now very aware of all aspects of his body is stressed through 'his eyes . . . his arms . . . his head . . . his stomach . . . his breath . . . his hand . . . his head . . . his gut'. There is almost a litany effect of this inventory of his body which serves to remind the reader of his physicality: a boy who is in acute pain. Magorian also uses the definitive article to show how alien Willie's surroundings are to him and to increase the reader's sympathy for the situation in which he finds himself. It is not 'his room' but 'the room'; he does not own it and therefore feels uncomfortable and uneasy in his situation. Even 'the eaves' provide a threat to him as he bashes his head, suggesting that, unless he has possession of what he encounters, he feels danger and unease. The only thing he really has ownership of is his own body, and this is painful to him as it has been so abused by others.

Nearly all the determiners used are definite and these very much give the impression that Willie is in a specific space, which clearly belongs to someone else. The only significant indefinite determiner used is about Willie's confusion that only dead people are 'laid out in a bed', when the use of 'a bed' creates even more unease as we realise his preoccupation with the threat of death all around him.

 ## Key Stage 4: *Never Let Me Go* by Kazuo Ishiguro

Extract from Chapter 6

What was so special about this song? Well, the thing was, I didn't used to listen properly to the words; I just waited for that bit that went: "Baby, baby, never let me go. . ." And what I'd imagine was a woman who'd been told that she couldn't have babies, who'd really, really wanted them all her life. Then there's a sort of miracle and she has a baby, and she holds this baby very close to her and walks around singing: "Baby, never let me go. . ." partly because she's so happy, but also because she's so afraid something will happen, that the baby will get ill or be taken away from her. Even at the times, I realised this couldn't be right, that this interpretation didn't fit with the rest of the lyrics. But that wasn't an issue with me. The song was about what I said, and I used to listen to it again and again, on my own, whenever I got the chance.

There was one strange incident around this time I should tell you about here. It really unsettled me, and although I wasn't able to find out its real meaning until years later, I think I sensed, even then, some deeper significance to it.

It was a sunny afternoon and I'd gone to our dorm to get something. I remember how bright it was because the curtains in our room hadn't been pulled back properly, and you could see the sun coming in in big shafts and see all the dust in the air. I hadn't meant to play the tape, but since I was there all by myself, an impulse made me get the cassette out of my collection box and put it into the player.

Maybe the volume had been turned right up by whoever had been using it last, I don't know. But it was much louder than I usually had it and that was probably why I didn't hear her before I did. Or maybe I'd just got complacent by then. Anyway, what I was doing was swaying about slowly in time to the song, holding an imaginary baby to my breast. In fact, to make it all the more embarrassing, it was one of those times I'd grabbed a pillow to stand in for the baby, and I was doing this slow dance, my eyes closed, singing softly [. . .]

(London: Faber and Faber, 2010, p.64)

> **WHY NOT CONSIDER?**
>
> ■ When is the author using a definite article and when is there use of the indefinite article?
> ■ What does this tell us about Kathy and how she approaches the song and dance?
> ■ How are we able to draw conclusions about her wishes for the future through her use of determiners?

Never Let Me Go is an interesting text for considering determiners, when so much of the novel concerns ownership as we discover gradually that the protagonist and her friends don't even have true ownership over their physical selves. The extract above considers the implications of the definite and indefinite determiners, and this gives an insight into the character and the impact that her communal life at Hailsham has had on her. At this point in the narrative, Kathy is describing the significance of a song on a tape and how it has continued to resonate through her life.

The extract begins with the demonstrative determiner in 'this song', which identifies for the reader that the song is significant to her. It isn't just 'a song': it is important and meaningful, and it identifies this as different to any other song, shown through the demonstrative determiner. Kathy continues with her narrative, constructing a meaning to 'this song' which she realises even at the time isn't entirely accurate, but her interesting use of the indefinite article when she refers to 'a sort of miracle and she has a baby' contributes to the vagueness that fits with her limited understanding. She knows – theoretically – that she won't be having children, so the haziness of the 'a sort of miracle' supports the sensation that Kathy still cannot fully define all her longings while maintaining some vagueness in the scenario as she uses her imagination as an escape from her future. The baby changes from 'a baby' to 'this baby' as she imagines holding her own, specific baby close in her arms, with the move from the indefinite article to a demonstrative determiner indicating that she is slipping into the role of a mother in her imagination. As she dives further into this wish-fulfilment fantasy the baby is now 'the baby', showing how substantial this baby has become to her as she loses herself in the fantasy.

The final paragraph moves from the indefinite article of 'an imaginary baby', as she begins the song and sinks into the scenario, until it becomes 'the baby', showing that the baby has become specific and real to her as she becomes further convinced by her imagined role as a mother. Although this might be a challenge for some students, the relationship between Kathy and her imagined baby shows us her longing for a 'normal' life and everything this could involve.

Key Stage 5: *Frankenstein* by Mary Shelley

Extract from Chapter 5

The different accidents of life are not so changeable as the feelings of human nature. I had worked hard for nearly two years, for the sole purpose of infusing life into an inanimate body. For this I had deprived myself of rest and health. I had desired it with an ardour that far exceeded moderation; but now that I had finished, the beauty of the dream vanished, and breathless horror and disgust filled my heart. Unable to endure the aspect of the being I had created, I rushed out of the room and continued a long time traversing my bedchamber, unable to compose my mind to sleep. At length lassitude succeeded to the tumult I had before endured, and I threw myself on the bed in my clothes, endeavouring to seek a few moments of forgetfulness. But it was in vain; I slept, indeed, but I was disturbed by the wildest dreams. I thought I saw Elizabeth, in the bloom of health, walking in the streets of Ingolstadt. Delighted and surprised, I embraced her, but as I imprinted the first kiss on her lips, they became livid with the hue of death; her features appeared to change, and I thought that I held the corpse of my dead mother in my arms; a shroud enveloped her form, and I saw the grave-worms crawling in the folds of the flannel. I started from my sleep with horror; a cold dew covered my forehead, my teeth chattered, and every limb became convulsed; when, by the dim and yellow light of the moon, as it forced its way through the window shutters, I beheld the wretch—the miserable monster whom I had created.

(Chicago and London: The University of Chicago Press, 1982, p.52)

> **WHY NOT CONSIDER?**
>
> - When does Shelley use 'an/a' and where does she use 'the'? Are there any contrasts or comparisons that could be made between her usage of indefinite and definite articles that might aid interpretation?
> - Is there a particular type of determiner used more often than others, and what might this reveal?

The first interesting use of a determiner in this passage, from Chapter 5 when Frankenstein's monster first comes alive, is when Frankenstein says 'the sole purpose of infusing life into an inanimate body'. The use of the indefinite article 'an' here could show the emotional detachment Frankenstein has towards his task. It is not a specific body with an identity and significance of its own; it is merely a general entity, more an abstract idea in some respects, and as such allows Frankenstein to detach himself completely from the horror of what he is doing. It is also interesting that Shelley uses 'an' to describe the body, as if the body were a whole, as Frankenstein uses a variety of parts to create his monster and not a single dead body. The fact that Frankenstein sees the deformed, composite creature as 'an' body – as opposed to 'things', which the collection of body parts surely should be described as – could demonstrate his disordered view of the world and the disturbing nature of his mind. What he sees as a whole, as a functioning body, is to anyone else nothing but a gross patchwork of limbs.

When describing his vivid dream of Elizabeth and her corpse-like features, Frankenstein only uses definite articles, grounding his dream in a very specific and clearly visualised reality. This could provide an interesting base for discussing Victor and how he views the world. His description of the dream and his description of the monster are both grounded in the same definite reality through his use of determiners, and students could explore what this says about Victor's state of mind, his grasp on reality, and how these factors influence his beliefs and decisions.

> **DEFINITE OR INDEFINITE?**
>
> The concept of indefinite and definite articles, revealing how a character feels towards an object or place, can be used effectively when looking at any prose text or poetry at Key Stage 5. Why not consider giving students a passage from a text and asking them to pick out the determiners, before challenging them to find the most interesting interpretation of their usage? This can be great practice for conducting close analysis and helping students find a range of interesting and less obvious meanings within a text. Focusing on determiners, which many students will think of as being entirely insignificant compared to other elements of language they could be looking at, also encourages them to keep their eyes open for the smaller details within language usage that often go unnoticed.

Creative writing

Students can be encouraged to think more carefully about how much information they choose to give to readers through their use of determiners. Determiners allow us to be specific or non-specific when discussing the details of situations, and it can be interesting to allow students to experiment with switching their use of definite and indefinite determiners, and pronouns with possessive determiners, to see what a difference this can make to a text to remove or add a sense of certainty.

As the rain began to pour down in sheets from the gloomy sky, she looked around for shelter. She saw a shop. Its lights were blazing, encouraging her to come closer and look at the delights within. She hesitated for a moment before opening the door and stepping into the warm, welcoming glow.

This account of coming across an unknown shop allows for a sense of mystery through the use of the indefinite determiner 'a' to describe the shop. The protagonist doesn't know or recognise the shop, and so neither do we. We do not know what it sells, either; all we know is that there are 'delights', and the use of the definite determiner 'the' to describe the 'delights' grounds them very much in reality. We know that the protagonist can see them, and so we are enticed into this mysterious shop just as much as she is. However, a subtle change in the usage of these determiners can change the mood of the extract entirely. Let's take a look:

A steady rain began to pour. She looked up, and then looked around. The shop appeared out of the darkness. Its lights blazed, drawing her to its shimmering windows, where a delight was promised to her if only she would step inside.

We still have exactly the same scenario here, but the change in determiners alters the mood and the expectations of the reader. The sentence starts with an indefinite determiner, lending a sense of uncertainty to the text from the beginning. We then have 'the shop' introduced. The fact that it is 'the' shop as opposed to 'a' shop suggests it is a place of significance: a place perhaps already known to the protagonist. This raises questions. Why is this specific shop so important? How does the protagonist already know of it? What role is it going to play? The delight here is framed within the context of an indefinite determiner, 'a', again posing questions. There is just one delight here, and we have no idea what it is; is it referring to the products on sale, or something else entirely? By using mainly indefinite determiners, everything in this extract takes on a sense of uncertainty and mystery. The definite determiner used to describe the shop, when placed within the context of the uncertainty around it, makes it even more mysterious as it is a specific place, a chosen place, and we do not know why.

Determiners may initially seem an insignificant element of the writing process, but, as can be seen through these examples, the subtle changes they make to the mood and atmosphere of texts can be very powerful. Focusing on such a small detail can be incredibly fruitful for students, particularly those who are more able and already confident writers. Having to pay such attention to detail can transform the quality of work students produce and show them how important even the most minor details of language can be when trying to produce a particular effect. With so much emphasis usually being put on adjectives when it comes to creative writing, it can also be very empowering for students who struggle with finding and/or using more abstract and complex words, such as EAL students or those with dyslexia, to realise that effective writing is not just down to how elaborate their vocabulary is, but also how careful they are about the seemingly minor details of language construction. If they know they can create a mood of uncertainty by simply changing determiners, rather than needing to look up words in a thesaurus, this can give them more confidence when it comes to approaching writing tasks.

SUGGESTED LESSON PLAN FOR KEY STAGE 4 ANALYSIS

This lesson plan is designed to be adaptable for any fiction text, hence we do not refer to any text in particular.

Equipment needed:
Photocopies of chosen extract/text
Highlighter pens
Strips of paper

L/O: To analyse the text creatively through exploring the use of determiners

> **LETTING GO OF LESSON OBJECTIVES**
>
> One of the joys of looking at texts from the perspective of grammar is that often both you and the students will end up looking at what have become very familiar sections of texts with new eyes. We are so often used to focusing on words and their variant meanings rather than their grammatical roles within a sentence; when the perspective of analysis is flipped, surprising and interesting discoveries suddenly appear out of texts we often think have nothing new to offer.
>
> As such, when starting to experiment with grammar-based analysis why not let go of lesson objectives in the sense of telling students what you want or expect them to find, and instead allow them to be textual explorers, free to discover whatever interests or intrigues them as they learn to look at language from a new angle? You might be surprised at what they find – and they probably will be, too, leading your lesson off into any number of fascinating directions that you couldn't have initially planned. Be bold and see where this approach leads you!

Starter (10 minutes)

(We would encourage you to check before you begin teaching that all students know what determiners are. If students are unsure, begin the lesson with a brief, evidenced explanation. If time is short, just focus on indefinite and definite determiners as these will probably prove the most fruitful to analyse.)

Hand out the photocopies of your chosen text/extract. Depending on the make-up of your class, and how used to close analysis they are, you could do this activity individually, in pairs or in small groups. Ask students to take a highlighter and highlight all the examples of determiners they can find. They then need to categorise them into definite or indefinite. Which are most common in the extract? Why do they think this might be? After five minutes or so, depending on the length of the extract and how long it will take them to read it closely, allow students to share their work with a peer/another pair/group and check they have found all the determiners. For more confident students, encourage them to check whether they have correctly differentiated between possessive determiners and pronouns. Then have a quick class feedback session to discuss which types of determiners are seen most frequently in the extract and what insight this might offer.

Main activity (35 minutes)

Task 1 (10 minutes): Ask students to look through the extract and find three examples of determiner usage they find interesting. Challenge them to come up with three one-sentence interpretations for these uses, clearly linked to the overall meaning of the text, and to write them down on three separate strips of paper. It is important that students clearly quote the sentence they are using as the basis of their interpretation. This task is best done individually to encourage independence, but if students are struggling then pair them up.

Task 2 (10 minutes): Ask students to swap their interpretation strips with other members of the class so they end up with three new interpretations. They should then find a partner and look at the six interpretations they have in front of them. Ask the students to discuss and evaluate the effectiveness of these interpretations, and choose the one they think is the most enlightening.

Task 3 (15 minutes): Ask students to now work in their pairs to take the one-sentence interpretation they like the best and turn it into a detailed paragraph that draws not just on the significance to the text as a whole but also to the context. What is this determiner actually doing in the text? What meaning does it have and how could it unlock deeper significance that may otherwise go unnoticed?

Plenary (15 minutes)

Ask pairs to share their chosen interpretation with the class, drawing out further areas of discussion and insight where appropriate. At the end of the sharing ask students to vote on their favourite interpretation, and consider how they might use determiners to come up with more subtle analytical points in future.

Differentiation

This task can be differentiated in several ways. The most basic is by amending individual tasks to becoming pair or small group tasks, allowing for more discussion and peer support if you feel the task is too challenging for some students to complete on their own.

Those who could benefit from an extra challenge could be given a more complex extract to look at, while those who may find this task more of a struggle could be given a simpler section of the extract with some specific questions/pointers to get them focusing on particular areas of the text immediately, rather than having to identify areas of interest by themselves. If you do decide to give different groups of students different texts, ensure they only swap interpretations with those who have been working on the same extract to prevent confusion.

Another way of challenging students with this type of task is to ask them to switch the type of determiner they can see in the sentence for its opposite, and consider what difference this might make. They could rewrite the extract, using the opposite determiners, and then share their findings with the class: does it change the meaning, and, if so, how? Does this offer them any deeper insight into the text?

Summing up

Determiners might seem small and insignificant, but we hope this chapter has shown you that even the tiniest elements of language construction can carry a great weight of meaning. Determiners are a fantastic element of grammar to use in activities to create more mindfulness in students of what is going on within texts. Paying attention to small details is where the moments of brilliance can come in literary analysis; spotting an incidence of 'the' rather than 'a' can open up a whole new interpretation that would otherwise be missed. Students alive to determiners are students who are alive to the minutiae, and we hope this will make them – and you – more vigilant and curious readers!

5 Punctuation

Punctuation is probably one of the greatest bugbears of an English teacher's life. No matter how frequently we teach students the correct usage of semicolons, colons and exclamation marks it seems that the theory can rarely be put into practice! Comma splices, subordinate clauses masquerading as main clauses, tentative semicolons chucked into sentences because they look clever – from Year 7 all the way up to Year 13, punctuation frustrates teachers and stumps students, restricting their ability to use it as both a creative and analytical tool. A solid grounding in punctuation can transform the quality of students' writing, enabling them to use it alongside careful vocabulary and grammar choices to create a range of effects. Understanding how they can use punctuation to liven up and add sophistication to their own writing also helps them to notice and articulate how writers are using it for effect in the texts they are studying.

> **WHERE SHOULD I START?**
>
> You might find it helpful to ensure students fully understand the difference between main and subordinate clauses (see Chapter One) before teaching punctuation, as once they can recognise these easily they should find it more straightforward to decide which punctuation marks they need.

Here is a breakdown of the functions of all the punctuation marks:

Commas

Commas are the default punctuation mark for most people. If in doubt, a comma seems to be considered the universal solution to all punctuation problems. As such, few students feel confident in explaining both the correct usage of commas and their actual function within a sentence. Many can talk about them being a pause in a sentence, but this is not necessarily a helpful descriptor as it doesn't enable students to differentiate between when they should use commas and when semicolons. Students need to be able to understand and articulate the theory behind the use of commas if they are going to use them correctly.

How commas work

Separating main and subordinate clauses:

As she was running late, she didn't eat breakfast.
I lived there for a while, though I didn't like it.

The most frequent mistake with commas is when students use them to separate two main clauses, creating a dreaded comma splice:

I went shopping, I bought three jumpers.

A method we use to explain when to use a comma is the idea of weakness and strength. A comma is a weak punctuation mark and can only hold a subordinate clause to a main clause. As soon as two main clauses want to come together, the comma becomes too weak and the sentence falls apart. As such, when you have two main clauses to join you need to use a semicolon, which is a strong punctuation mark and can withstand the weight of two main clauses either side of it. A nice visual way to show this is by drawing a comma and adding the dot above to turn it into a semicolon: adding something to it shows how it is becoming stronger. You can also help students to remember the difference in strength between a comma and a semicolon by pointing out that a semicolon contains a full stop and a comma doesn't. Therefore a semicolon can replace a full stop and a comma can't.

Relative clauses, where the information isn't necessary to the sentence, are marked within the sentence by pairs of commas:

Amir, who was running late that morning, left home without his lunch.

As 'who was running late that morning' is a **non-restrictive relative clause** (see Chapter One, Sentences) it needs commas to separate it from the rest of the sentence. If the clause were taken away, the rest of the sentence (*Amir left home without his lunch*) would still make perfect sense, which is a way for students to work out whether they have used the commas in the correct place. It may also help to explain to students that if you could use brackets to close off a particular part of a sentence then a pair of commas will do exactly the same job.

Restrictive relative clauses (that begin with who, which, that, whom or where), however, do not need commas as the information given in the relative clause is essential to the meaning of the sentence:

Passengers who need assistance with their bags should go to the customer service desk.

Here the restrictive relative clause, 'who need assistance with their bags', is entirely necessary to the sentence in order for it to make sense, and, as such, commas should not be used.

To mark off an aside:

Commas are also used to mark off unnecessary parts of a sentence that do not form a sentence clause. These are usually asides, providing extra information that could be removed easily without detracting from the meaning of the sentence:

> *Atifa had, just like last year, forgotten Tom's birthday.*
> *He had written a book, Halfway to Heaven, that had been a huge success.*

Separating items in a list:
Commas should be used to separate more than two items in a list:

> *I bought apples, eggs, some bread and a pint of milk.*

With however:
Commas should always be used after however when however means 'by contrast' or 'on the other hand'. When it means 'in whatever way', you should not use a comma:

> *However, several people will need to arrive early in order to ensure things run smoothly on the day.*
> *However, Sarah didn't think it would be necessary to call him.*
> *However she tried to fix the problem, it still wouldn't work.*
> *However likely it may have been, there still was no guarantee.*

The Oxford comma:
The Oxford comma refers to the optional comma that can be used after the penultimate item in a list of three or more items, before 'and' or 'or'.

Semicolons

Semicolons seem to induce fear in many people, and understanding when to use them can be quite tricky. As referenced before, using the idea of weakness and strength works well when discussing the differences between commas and semicolons, as semicolons are specifically used for separating two main clauses that are connected by subject matter:

> *I told her not to go out in the rain; she didn't listen.*
> *There were so many she didn't know what to do with them; Jake said he'd take some home with him.*

Semicolons can be replaced by full stops or conjunctions, which provides an easy way for students to stop and check for themselves whether they have used them correctly if they're not confident with identifying main and subordinate clauses. If a full stop or conjunction wouldn't work, then their semicolon should (in most cases) be a comma.

Colons

Colons are used before a list of two or more items, a quotation or an explanation. They are different from semicolons by not needing to join two main clauses; the explanation following a colon does not need to be a full sentence to be grammatically correct:

> *Priya knew whom she should have asked for help instead: Max.*
> *The classrooms had been painted over the summer: white for English and pale blue for Maths.*
> *There were five things they needed to remember to buy: torches, rope, tent poles, batteries and sleeping bags.*
> *Sam's mum always said: 'If in doubt, go without.'*

Full stops

Full stops should only ever be used at the end of a complete sentence. Some students struggle with where to put a full stop when writing speech; full stops in this case should always come before the final inverted comma(s).

Question marks

Question marks indicate when a direct or rhetorical question is being asked. When used with direct speech, the question mark should be inside the inverted comma(s). A question mark has the same function as a full stop in that it ends a sentence, and any word coming afterwards should begin with a capital letter.

Exclamation marks

Exclamation marks are very popular with students and are frequently overused in their writing. It is important to stress to students that exclamation marks are used to express shock, surprise, amusement or the loudness of someone's voice, and should certainly not be used at the end of every sentence! Exclamation marks are, like full stops and question marks, considered to denote the end of a sentence and so any word following on from an exclamation mark should begin with a capital letter.

Inverted commas (quotation marks)

Inverted commas are used to punctuate direct or reported speech, or to quote from texts. There is no hard-and-fast rule as to whether to use double or single inverted commas, though the usual British convention is to use single inverted commas unless quoting within a quote, in which case double are used. However, American English is the opposite and many students may be more familiar with using double inverted commas for speech if they have been taught that way in the past. It is perfectly correct to use whatever students feel comfortable with; it is just important that they remain consistent in their style throughout a text. All punctuation of what is quoted within inverted commas, whether double or single, needs to be placed before the final inverted comma.

Hyphens and dashes

Hyphens and dashes can often look identical, but they have very different uses.

Hyphens are used to join two words or parts of words together to make a compound word or phrase. Compound adjectives such as 'long-term' or 'rust-coloured', when used before a noun, are modifying the noun and so need a hyphen. If used after the noun, they don't. For example:

The rust-coloured wall fitted in perfectly to the surrounding desert landscape. (Here 'rust-coloured' is modifying 'wall', hence the need for the hyphen.)

She knew she was in it for the long term. (Here 'long term' is not modifying anything, so it doesn't need a hyphen.)

Dashes are used to indicate a pause in the sentence and can replace brackets, commas and even semicolons in informal writing. They are particularly effective in creative writing tasks when wanting to express a chatty, breathless voice in direct or reported speech – see Miss Bates' speech in Jane Austen's *Emma* for an excellent example.

Brackets

Brackets are used to mark asides or give additional information that isn't necessary to a sentence. If brackets and the information within them were removed from the sentence, the rest of the sentence should still make sense. Pairs of commas or dashes, depending on preference, can replace brackets. Punctuation marks should be within the brackets unless the brackets end the sentence, in which case the final punctuation mark should go outside the brackets:

Sarah (who I hated so much!) was the last person to get on the coach, and the seat next to mine was the only one left (just my luck).

Putting it into practice

Now we have covered the different forms and categories of the major types of punctuation that will be found in texts, we will explore how analysis of them will create a deeper understanding of authorial intentions in literature. This segment has been split by Key Stage and also includes a section on creative writing.

Key Stage 3: *A Monster Calls* by Patrick Ness

Extract from Chapter One

The monster showed up just after midnight. As they do.
   Conor was awake when it came.
   He'd had a nightmare. Well, not a nightmare. The nightmare. The one he'd been having a lot lately. The one with the darkness and the wind and the screaming. The one with the hands slipping from his grasp, no matter how hard he tried to hold on. The one that always ended with—
   "Go away," Conor whispered into the darkness of his bedroom, trying to push the nightmare back, not let it follow him into the world of waking.
                                      (London: Walker Books, 2012, p.15)

A Monster Calls is a fantastic book to study at Key Stage 3 because of its sensitive and powerful treatment of grief and the role of the imagination in how we deal with emotions. Though told in the third person, the voice of Conor, the male protagonist, is vivid and realistic. This opening section of the novel is intriguing in many ways and the use of punctuation is key in quickly building the suspense required to hook the reader. While there are several grammatical features of interest in this paragraph, we're going to focus on the use of punctuation and what interpretations we might be able to draw from it at this early stage in the novel.

> **WHY NOT CONSIDER?**
>
> ■ What effect do the full stops have? Is this the only way suspense is created in this opening section?
> ■ What effect does the interspersing of long and short sentences have?
> ■ There is a lot of non-standard grammar in this section – how would you address this with students?

Students should be able to see quite easily in this opening section that there are a lot of short sentences, where the only punctuation is a full stop. Students could perhaps start by highlighting how many full stops there are in this paragraph, and then consider what the amount of full stops might signify. The notion that short, simple sentences create suspense is something familiar to most children by the end of primary school; it is important that they can articulate why this is, however. The lack of information given in short sentences and the constant pausing they require of the reader function as a restrictive force, as a gate-keeper if you like, pushing us back and keeping us at arm's length from the story. We are being prevented at every turn from finding out more, and it is this obstructive quality that makes full stops so effective when used frequently in a short text. There is more that could be said on this, however; rather than stopping at suspense, how much further could students take their interpretations? The passage is describing a nightmare; why might this be a particularly suitable topic with which to use a sequence of short sentences with lots of full stops? Within the context of a nightmare, the full stops could be a metaphorical representation of the obstructive nature of bad dreams, in terms of their confusing and disorienting subject matter as well as their habit of abruptly waking us from our sleep. The full stops are more than just punctuation here: they are also arguably a physical reminder, printed on the page, of how nightmares, too, stop us in our tracks and prevent us from sleeping.

This idea of obstruction continues with the use of the dash in the middle of the sentence that is almost about to tell us how the dream ends. By cutting off the sentence like this, suspense is built as we will have to wait longer to know what exactly is haunting Conor's dreams. However, it also allows us to step into the nightmare world more effectively as our own nightmares are often truncated by being woken suddenly. Not being able to finish the dream, to have a resolution, is what contributes to making nightmares so psychologically haunting. In this extract, moving beyond simplistic comments about building tension is important; students must understand how the author, Patrick Ness, is cleverly using punctuation to recreate for the reader the experience of being in a nightmare.

This extract is also worth using for a fruitful discussion of how sometimes writers break the rules of grammar. There are plenty of subordinate clauses being used as main clauses in this section, and some students may be confused as to why this is 'allowed' in a book but not in their own writing. You will probably have your own ways of explaining this in your classrooms, and there is certainly no right or wrong way of exploring this issue. However, we find it useful to talk to students about how writers strive to create realistic and lively voices in their writing, and that, as we often don't talk in complete, grammatical sentences in everyday conversation, writers have to bend the rules slightly in order to echo normal speech patterns and make sure their words read naturally off the page. Giving students the chance to do this in their own creative writing can be a good way of enabling them to experiment with breaking the rules, while ensuring they recognise that formal writing obviously requires them to use standard grammatical conventions.

Key Stage 4: *Pride and Prejudice* by Jane Austen

Extract from Volume 1, Chapter 1

> "Why, my dear, you must know, Mrs Long says that Netherfield is taken by a young man of large fortune from the north of England; that he came down on Monday in a chaise and four to see the place, and was so much delighted with it that he agreed with Mr Morris immediately; that he is to take possession before Michaelmas, and some of his servants are to be in the house by the end of next week."
>
> "What is his name?"

"Bingley."

"Is he married or single?"

"Oh! single, my dear, to be sure! A single man of large fortune; four or five thousand a year. What a fine thing for our girls!"

"How so? how can it affect them?"

"My dear Mr Bennet," replied his wife, "how can you be so tiresome! You must know that I am thinking of his marrying one of them."

"Is that his design in settling here?"

"Design! Nonsense, how can you talk so! But it is very likely that he may fall in love with one of them, and therefore you must visit him as soon as he comes."

"I see no occasion for that. You and the girls may go, or you may send them by themselves, which perhaps will be still better; for, as you are as handsome as any of them, Mr Bingley might like you the best of the party."

(London: Penguin, 2003, p.6)

This famous opening section of *Pride and Prejudice* gives us a wonderfully humorous insight into the Bennet's marriage, as well as Mrs Bennet's desperation to see her daughters married. The dialogue reveals much about the two Bennet parents' characters and their opposing ways of viewing the world. Much of this opposition can be explored through the contrasting punctuation they employ in their speech, making a close study of this text through punctuation a rewarding exercise for students at Key Stage 4.

> **WHY NOT CONSIDER?**
>
> - When does Mrs Bennet use exclamation marks and when not? What does her use of exclamation marks tell us about her personality?
> - What punctuation is most frequently used when Mr Bennet speaks? What could this reveal about his personality?
> - How does punctuation set up the two Bennets as opposites?

Tracking this extract through from beginning to end, there are plenty of interesting observations to be made about how Jane Austen reveals character through her use of punctuation. Starting with Mrs Bennet's announcement of Netherfield being let at last, Austen's use of semicolons and commas in Mrs Bennet's speech allows us to understand the rhythm of her voice. Her frequent pauses to breathe and additions of unnecessary information after each semicolon reveal both her gossipy nature and her excitement at the prospect of a new man in the neighbourhood. We immediately know, therefore, that we are being introduced to a woman who does not act in the way we would expect of a wife of a clergyman, or the mother of five almost grown daughters. Mr Bennet's responses to his wife's ebullience also reveal much about his nature; the short, teasing, ironic questions he asks function merely to fan the flames of her enthusiasm, and he clearly takes pleasure in winding her up. The intellectual gulf between the couple is shown through the punctuation used; Mr Bennet's wry, ironic tone is juxtaposed with the breathless enthusiasm of Mrs Bennet's exclamation marks, a punctuation mark the unruffled Mr Bennet does not use at all.

It is also interesting to note when Mrs Bennet doesn't use exclamation marks; her sentences that are short and merely use full stops are spoken as calm facts. The rather ridiculous-sounding 'but it is very likely that he may fall in love with one of them, and therefore you must visit him as soon as he comes' is not something that needs an exclamation mark, because Mrs Bennet sees it as quite a settled reality. Her state of mind is therefore revealed by her punctuation. Her exclamation marks show how excitable she is and how easily riled by her husband's teasing, while her full stops show how her vision of one of her daughters already being mistress of Netherfield appears so real to her that she can talk about it as if it were indisputable.

What adjectives could therefore be drawn from this use of punctuation to describe Mrs Bennet? Her immaturity is certainly something that can be inferred from this punctuation use, as well as her naïvety. Even though she will eventually be proven right in her surmises, Austen's presentation of Mrs Bennet here through her punctuation usage could perhaps suggest to us that this correct prediction is nothing to do with her intelligence. For more able students, this is an opportunity to look at what Austen is saying about the roles of mothers and fathers, and how differently they parent. While we can laugh at Mrs Bennet, is Mr Bennet's wry questioning any more effective an approach to addressing the issue of his daughters' very real precariousness in a situation where marriage is their only hope for a secure future? The opposing punctuation may initially make it seem that Austen is merely poking fun at Mrs Bennet, but more observant students may want to consider what Austen could be saying by having Mr Bennet dismiss and ridicule his wife through his ironic questioning. This arguably reveals his lack of understanding of how important these questions, treated merely as a jest, really are. His wry question marks appear far less intelligent when we realise that he is not taking his daughter's future prospects seriously; a single man in the village must surely be something that affects them, for how else will they be able to live independently if they don't try to attract a suitable mate? Who, then, is really the fool here, and how can the punctuation help us to justify our answers?

 ## Key Stage 5: *Birdsong* by Sebastian Faulks

Extract from Part Six

Stephen put away his pen and notebook. It was night-time. There was moonlight on the hills above the village. He lit another cigarette and turned the pages of a magazine. There was a pile by the chair of others he had already skimmed. His eyes scanned each page but barely read.

He went outside into the yard behind the little house. Chickens scattered in front of his footsteps.

He went into the lane and began to walk. The road was half made up. He felt the puddles and the loose stones beneath his feet. He went as far as the main road and looked around him. The guns were soft and distant; they rumbled like a train going through an embankment.

(London: Vintage, 1994, p.425)

Faulks' contemporary time-shifting First World War novel is a popular choice with many exam boards at A Level. It is a structurally interesting novel in the way Faulks changes his language between the three time periods the novel crosses – pre-war, war and the reasonably modern day – as well as providing students with plenty to consider when it comes to issues such as the purpose of war, legacy and memory. Punctuation can have a key role in analysis when studying *Birdsong* due to the importance of the distinctive stylistic shifts that signal the changes in time and point of view. Looking at how Faulks chooses to change his sentence structures depending on the era, and through whose eyes he is telling the story, can offer some useful opportunities for students to show their understanding of the role of language and structure in shaping meaning: key to exam success.

> **WHY NOT CONSIDER?**
>
> ■ What is the role of the full stop here? What could we say about the full stop apart from the creation of short sentences?
> ■ What purpose does the semicolon in the final sentence have? What significance is there in the fact that this sentence has a semicolon whereas all the others around it do not?
> ■ How might the use of the full stop allow insight into both setting and character?

When teaching at sixth form level it can be useful to start a lesson with a short, challenging analysis task that gets students thinking. Why not try taking this extract and asking students to see what meanings they can draw from the punctuation, either individually or in pairs, before going through it together as a class? Or, for something a little more interesting, take the extract and remove all punctuation and capital letters and get the students to punctuate it as they see fit, before showing them the original. This can be very revealing in showing where conventional or logical punctuation structures haven't been followed by the writer, highlighting deliberate adaptations that can provide clues to deeper meanings.

This extract, almost at the end of the novel, is set in 1918. Students can use the full stops here as a way of understanding the mindset of Stephen as he enters his fifth year of fighting. The constant stops could have a number of different meanings: the way in which Stephen's life has come to a halt; the way in which his mind is no longer able to think of anything, any future, beyond the immediate day, or the way in which the war has deadened his feelings and made him incapable of connecting with anyone in a meaningful way. Students can then be encouraged to consider what tone the constant full stops produce. Reading aloud can be helpful to allow students to hear the effect: it is disruptive, monotonous. This could reflect the emotional impact of war but could also echo the marching of feet, the monotone landscape of no-man's land; students can be free to experiment with their interpretations and see what they come up with.

The use of the semicolon in the final sentence is very interesting and could allow for some sophisticated analysis. Ordinarily a sentence with a semicolon wouldn't be worth paying much attention to, but when it is the only semicolon among a sea of full stops it's worth sitting up and noticing. This sentence, 'the guns were soft and distant; they rumbled like a train going through an embankment', offers us a contrast in its two main clauses; the world of war and the world of peace, where trains rumble peacefully through the landscape. The former clause is the current reality; the latter both harks back to a peaceful past and hints at a peaceful future. After all, we are introduced to Elizabeth, Stephen's granddaughter, when she is on a Tube train some 60 years in the future, and the image of the train and the militaristic vocabulary used to describe it are repeatedly employed as a link between the two time periods. This use of a semicolon arguably functions as a microcosm of the entire novel, which is all about the constant presence of the past and the impossibility of separating it from the present. Even this everyday, seemingly innocuous image of a train has become sullied by association with war; the war has crept into every part of Stephen's memory and consciousness, and he will never be able to leave it behind, even when peace finally comes.

 ## Creative writing

Being able to confidently use all types of punctuation in writing, and understand the subtle differences in function and effect between them, gives students the freedom to be more creative in their work. Rather than relying solely on the vocabulary they use, they can start experimenting with structure, adding more sophistication and style, as well as developing their own voices while being able to realistically create the voices of characters.

A way into experimenting with punctuation can be through restricting its use. Asking students to write a short descriptive passage only using full stops, or only using commas and full stops, or semicolons and full stops, can be an interesting way for them to see what happens when they can't use a particular punctuation mark and how that affects the feel of their writing. This exclusion technique can work really well when trying to help students understand when to use punctuation accurately: commas being the most common mistake, banning them altogether can help students see more clearly the difference between them and semicolons.

Another activity that can work well to show the effect of punctuation is to have students write a scene only using full stops and then, underneath, rewrite the scene using a wider range of punctuation. Comparing and contrasting the tone of these scenes should reveal to them how the punctuation they use has an integral role to play in creating an appropriate atmosphere.

Having fun with creating characters is another way to bring punctuation into creative writing. You could show students some images of people and ask them to write a short scene of dialogue between the people, using punctuation to bring out their personalities. Which type of person might use short sentences in their speech, and which dashes? Showing them how punctuation can bring someone's voice alive also reveals the benefits of understanding and using punctuation correctly. This type of activity could be coupled with a drama task; having students script and perform their characters, thinking very carefully about how exactly they want lines said, can hone their precision when using punctuation.

Modelling collective creative work on the board and allowing students to come up and move punctuation around, replace punctuation and delete punctuation, and then discuss the effect of this, can be a useful way to support students who are not as confident with their writing. This type of activity can also work in smaller groups, when students work together to produce something effective using large sheets of paper or mini whiteboards. If you have enough space in your classroom you can also use the children themselves as punctuation. Have a row of students standing up, each holding a word, and form them into a sentence. Then ask one student to represent a comma, one a semicolon, one a full stop and so on, and ask them to stand between the words they think they should separate. The rest of the class can then have fun shouting out suggestions as to where their friends should move to make the sentence even better.

SUGGESTED KEY STAGE 3 LESSON PLAN

Equipment needed:
Excerpts from texts

L/O: To use punctuation for effect in creative writing

Starter (10 minutes)

Students can work in small groups to look at excerpts from texts, with each group examining the same texts. Ask students to identify which punctuation is being used, and what effect it has, before sharing their ideas with the whole class; does everyone think the same about each text? Get students to pull their ideas together and see whether they think each punctuation mark has a specific effect or whether this changes, depending on the context.

Main activity (30 minutes)

Put up a PowerPoint slide with a table containing three columns, labelled setting, atmosphere and punctuation. There should be several choices in each column, as below:

Setting	Atmosphere	Punctuation
Luxury hotel	Peaceful	Full stop
Abandoned mansion	Lively	Comma
Beach	Disturbing	Semicolon

Students can then mix and match from the table, picking a setting, atmosphere and punctuation to use in their writing. If you know particular students are struggling with a type of punctuation you may wish to make them use that punctuation in order to develop their confidence with it. Students should then write a paragraph, trying to create the setting and atmosphere they have chosen through the use of the punctuation they have picked (they do not only have to use that punctuation, but they should make an effort to use the punctuation mark in all, or most, sentences).

Once they have been writing for 15 minutes, ask students to swap their work with a partner without telling them what options they picked from the table. Their partner then has to see whether they can guess correctly which options their peer chose. Students should feed back their findings to the class and consider whether, if some students struggled with expressing their chosen atmosphere, it was because the punctuation they picked didn't help them create the right effect.

Using the feedback from the whole class and their partner, students should then rewrite their paragraph, changing their choice of punctuation, if necessary, to create a stronger piece with a clearer atmosphere.

Plenary (10 minutes)

Encourage selected students to read their work aloud. The class can then give collective feedback, thinking about how punctuation specifically creates effects. Students can be prompted to summarise what they have learned, either orally or in writing, about the role punctuation has to play in creating atmosphere.

Differentiation

This lesson can be differentiated easily by allowing students to work in small groups or pairs if they need more support, or individually for those who would benefit from a challenge. For the starter activity, those students who are very confident could work together on analysing others' extracts and summarising their own findings to present to the class, rather than taking part in the whole-class discussion.

For the free writing portion of the lesson, less confident students can be supported with sentence starters to get them going. Those who are struggling, or who are at the early stages of learning English, could be given a partially written paragraph that they can add to, or a paragraph that has been almost entirely written and that they merely need to punctuate.

SUGGESTED KEY STAGE 4/5 LESSON PLAN

This lesson plan is designed to be adaptable for any text, and so we mention none in particular.

Equipment needed:
Unpunctuated extracts for students to annotate

L/O: To analyse a text, considering how structure creates meaning

Starter (15 minutes)

Start the lesson by giving students a key extract from the text they are studying, with all punctuation and capital letters removed. Students can do this activity individually or in pairs, depending on their confidence level. They are then instructed to try and fill in the punctuation and capital letters according to what they feel would make sense and be grammatically correct. When they are finished, students can partner with another individual or pair to compare their extracts. Have they used the same punctuation or are there differences? Where there are differences, how can they each justify their choices? You should then project the unpunctuated extract onto the board and ask students to say where the punctuation should be and what type; any areas where there are disagreements should prompt discussion as to why/how the final choice has been made. When finished making the class version you should then show the actual extract and highlight any areas of difference. These areas should be pointed out as showing a deliberate device on behalf of the author to choose unexpected punctuation, and students should be encouraged to discuss why that might be and what effect it has.

Note: this starter activity works best with a short extract – i.e. no more than six lines. If a longer extract analysis is desired for more challenging work, this activity could easily expand to fit an entire lesson.

Main (35 minutes)

Using the skills they have just learned from the starter activity, ask students to choose a key moment from the text they are studying and, either individually or in pairs, look closely at the punctuation. Applying the notion of what would be logical punctuation to what the writer has chosen, they should highlight any areas of punctuation within the extract that seem unusual or interesting. Thinking carefully about the content of those sentences and the context of the text around it, they should then come up with three possible interpretations of the punctuation usage, recording their ideas either in books or on post-it notes.

When finished, students should swap their extracts with a partner and repeat the process with the new extract. When both partners have completed the task they should put together their separate interpretations of the same extract and compare and contrast their ideas. At this point you can be circling the classroom to guide and add to students' interpretations if you feel this to be appropriate.

After time for paired discussions, the students should then be encouraged to share their general findings in a whole-class setting, highlighting any particularly enlightening interpretations they have gained through the activity. It would be wise to encourage students to write down any especially noteworthy ideas for future reference.

Plenary (15 minutes)

Using their original extract, students should now consolidate their learning through writing an analytical paragraph to explore their ideas about the effect of the punctuation in their chosen area of the text.

Differentiation

The easiest way to differentiate this task is to pre-prepare extracts that range in difficulty and be strategic about who works on which extract. Students who can cope with more challenge could be given longer extracts, where the punctuation is not particularly obvious in having a stylistic purpose, to make them really think when it comes to analysis. Those who will find the task more of a struggle can be given a shorter extract, where the punctuation has a clear purpose in creating a specific mood.

Students can be grouped strategically for a task of this nature, allowing for pairings or groupings that can support one another. For more challenge, all of the tasks in this lesson can be done individually.

To provide more support, students could be given 'prompt' questions – such as, 'are the full stops preventing us from finding out any information?' – which will help them spot features they may struggle to identify. Prompts could also be used for more challenge, posing 'what if?' questions – such as, 'what if the semicolon in sentence three were removed?'

Summing up

Punctuation is about so much more than following rules, and we hope this chapter has shown how it can be used both creatively and analytically to enrich students' understanding of its vital role in creating meaning. Rather than being a dry area of grammar that causes headaches, punctuation, when divorced from the notion of being 'correct' or 'incorrect', becomes something fun that can be played around and experimented with, and a fun, clue-hunting activity within texts to uncover hidden authorial meanings. When approached with this more creative, active-based mindset, we find that students' attitudes change considerably. Why not give this a go and see what you can do with punctuation in your classroom?

6 Extension vocabulary (or 'wow' words!)

Students can often have analytical ideas about literature that are highly sophisticated, yet they lack the vocabulary to accurately express them. By giving students the specific terminology they need to examine these ideas, they become confident enough to spot patterns in the texts they are studying and identify the grammatical features. Even from the start of Key Stage 3, many students are ready to tackle complex literary terminology, embrace the challenge of recognising these terms when they are put into practice in texts, and then consider the significance of the choices made and their frequency. By Key Stage 4, the ability to use complex vocabulary gives a polish and sophistication to students' writing that will lift their confidence as they approach public examinations, and all Key Stage 5 students will find their understanding of the terms are fully embedded as they embark on A-Level work.

Alliteration	Repetition of the same consonant sounds, usually at the start of words	'Deep into that darkness peering, long I stood there wondering, fearing, Doubting, dreaming dreams no mortal ever dared to dream before' **The Raven by Edgar Allen Poe**
Anaphora	The deliberate repetition of the first part of the sentence in order to achieve an artistic effect	'It was the best of times, it was the worst of times, it was the age of wisdom, it was the age of foolishness, it was the epoch of belief, it was the epoch of incredulity, it was the season of Light, it was the season of Darkness, it was the spring of hope, it was the winter of despair' **A Tale of Two Cities by Charles Dickens**

Assonance	Repetition or a pattern of the same vowel sounds	'From folk that sat on the terrace and drew out the even' long / Sudden crowings of laughter, monotonous drone of song' ***Ballads* by Robert Louis Stevenson**
Anthropomorphism	The attribution of human characteristics to a god, animal or object – not abstract concepts (this is personification)	'But at my back I always hear / Time's winged chariot drawing near' ***To His Coy Mistress* by Andrew Marvell**
Antithesis	A rhetorical device in which two opposite ideas are put together in a sentence for contrasting effect	'Good we must love, and must hate ill, For ill is ill, and good good still' ***Community* by John Donne**
Antimetabole	When a phrase or sentence is repeated in reverse order for effect, without changing the meaning	'Fair is foul and foul is fair, hover through the fog and filthy air' ***Macbeth* by William Shakespeare**
Caesura	A pause in a line of poetry, often – but not always – signified through punctuation	'Dead! One of them shot by the sea in the east… What art can a woman be good at? Oh, vain!' ***Mother and Poet* by Elizabeth Barrett Browning**
Chiasmic structure	The reversing of the order of words in the second of two parallel phrases, maintaining the grammatical structure of the original sentence. All examples of antimetabole are also examples of chiasmus, but the reverse is not true as a chiasmic sentence can have its meaning changed through the reversal of words	'Ask not what your country can do for you, but what you can do for your country' **J F Kennedy** (by using chiasmus, and not antimetabole, the meaning of the second sentence is changed from the first despite using the same words in reverse order)
Connotations	An associated meaning of a word/image/object	'Shall I compare thee to a summer's day?' ***Sonnet 18* by William Shakespeare**

Consonance	The repetition of a consonant sound in consecutive or nearby words	'And fit the bright steel-pointed sock' **Follower by Seamus Heaney**
Enjambment	A line ending, in which the sense continues (with no punctuation) into the following line or stanza	'April is the cruellest month, breeding Lilacs out of the dead land, mixing Memory and desire, stirring Dull roots with spring rain' **The Waste Land by T S Eliot**
Epizeuxis	The repetition of a word or phrase in immediate succession for effect	'Tomorrow and tomorrow and tomorrow' **Macbeth by William Shakespeare**
Hyperbaton	When the normal order of words is inverted for effect	'Some rise by sin, and some by virtue fall' **Measure for Measure by William Shakespeare**
Hyperbole	Exaggeration for effect	'Neptune's ocean wash this blood Clean from my hand? No. This my hand will rather The multitudinous seas incarnadine, Making the green one red' **Macbeth by William Shakespeare**
Half-rhyme	Two lines that end with words that nearly rhyme	'If love is like a bridge Or maybe like a grudge' **To my Wife by George Wolff**
Iambic pentameter	A poetic meter where each line has ten syllables with alternating stress	'If music be the food of love, play on; Give me excess of it, that, surfeiting, The appetite may sicken, and so die' **Twelfth Night by William Shakespeare**
Imagery	Using figurative language to represent objects, ideas and actions in such a way that it appeals to our physical senses	'Hedge-crickets sing; and now with treble soft The redbreast whistles from a garden-croft, And gathering swallows twitter in the skies' **To Autumn by John Keats**

Metaphor	When a writer portrays a person, place, thing or an action as *being* something else, even though it is not *actually* that something else	'It is the East and Juliet is the sun' ***Romeo and Juliet* by William Shakespeare**
Metonymy	A figure of speech when something is called by a new name that is related to the original meaning or concept	'The pen is mightier than the sword' ***Richelieu: Or the Conspiracy* by Edward Bulwer-Lytton** (Here 'the pen' means literature and 'the sword' means violence)
Onomatopoeia	A figure of speech in which words are used to imitate sounds	'The moan of doves in immemorial elms, And murmuring of innumerable bees' ***The Princess* by Alfred, Lord Tennyson**
Oxymoron	A figure of speech in which two opposite ideas are joined to create an effect	'Why, then, O brawling love! O loving hate! O anything, of nothing first create!' ***Romeo and Juliet* by William Shakespeare**
Pathetic fallacy	A literary device that attributes human qualities and emotions to inanimate objects of nature	'The night has been unruly. Where we lay, Our chimneys were blown down and, as they say, Lamentings heard i' th' air, strange screams of death, And prophesying with accents terrible Of dire combustion and confused events New hatched to the woeful time.' ***Macbeth* by William Shakespeare**
Personification	A figure of speech in which non-human things or abstract ideas are given human attributes	'When well-apparelled April on the heel Of limping winter treads' ***Romeo and Juliet* by William Shakespeare**

Parallelism	The use of components in a sentence that are grammatically the same or similar in their construction	'To err is human; to forgive divine' **An Essay on Criticism by Alexander Pope**
Sibilance	The repetition of the 'sh' or 's' sounds	'Sweet dreams, form a shade O'er my lovely infants head. Sweet dreams of pleasant streams By happy silent moony beams Sweet sleep with soft down' **Songs of Innocence and Experience by William Blake**
Simile	When a writer draws comparisons with the use of 'like' or 'as'	'Tormenting itself in its invincible ignorance like a small bird beating about the cruel wires of a cage' **Lord Jim by Joseph Conrad**
Synaesthesia	A technique to present ideas, characters or places in such a manner that they appeal to more than one sense, such as hearing, seeing, smelling etc., at a given time	'Tasting of Flora and the country green Dance, and Provencal song, and sun burnt mirth!' **Ode to a Nightingale by John Keats**
Synecdoche	This is very similar to metonymy but specifically relates to a phrase where a part of something is substituted for the whole	'The western wave was all a-flame, The day was well-nigh done!' **The Rime of the Ancient Mariner by Samuel Taylor Coleridge** (Here the sea is substituted for 'western wave')
Triadic structure	Words or phrases grouped in threes for emphasis or rhythm.	'The parachute flopped and banged and pulled' **Lord of the Flies by William Golding**
Zoomorphism	The attribution of animal characteristics to humans or objects	'Lennie dabbled his big paw in the water' **Of Mice and Men by John Steinbeck**

This section of the book examines terminology that is broadly appropriate for each Key Stage, although we find that exceptional students are ready to use some surprisingly advanced grammatical features. As their confidence with the vocabulary increases, so will your ability to teach complex ideas and reinforce in students the belief that they can interpret texts in very astute ways. The chapter is more activity-orientated than others in the book, and many of the activities have been designed to be adapted for use as starter or revision tasks.

Putting it into practice

 Key Stage 3

During this Key Stage students are faced, often for the first time, with some very ambitious vocabulary that equips them to write about and understand poetry and prose in a more structured and formal way than perhaps the more instinctive approach they will have encountered at primary school. We have always found Years 7 to 9 to be incredibly receptive to new terminology, and many students are delighted to learn challenging terms that allow them to explore literary works in a more sophisticated way. It is, however, important not to overload them with new and exciting terminology as this can make some students become 'spotters' rather than analysers. It is fantastic to see a class being able to recognise assonance or enjambment and showing that they clearly understand the definitions, but it is of limited benefit to students if they do not pause to think what these convey to the reader. We always stress the need for AO2, even to those in Key Stage 3, so that students become accustomed to considering how the use of a device has had an impact or why it was selected by the writer.

Very often the easiest way for students to become familiar and confident with new terminology is through the study of poetry, where the condensed and rich nature of the language can offer a wide range of examples. It also has the benefit of students not being distracted by plot or character action, as in a novel, so that they can link their application of terminology, and analysis of the effect, to a single line or stanza and not become overwhelmed in considering how this applies to a wider text.

We are going to look at two poems for Key Stage 3, to explore some terminology and to suggest how students might want to consider the impact it has on their understanding of certain sections and on the poems as a whole. 'Blackberry Picking' by Seamus Heaney and 'Mametz Wood' by Owen Sheers are modern works which are readily available and very accessible to this age group.

Enjambment

This can be an excellent starting point for discussion, and the really visual nature of this device makes it a great confidence booster for anyone who feels a little unsure or timorous about poetry analysis. The very simple question, 'Does the end of the sentence happen at the end of the line of poetry, or does it carry on?', is straightforward to work out, and giving students coloured pens so they can annotate a copy of the poem and literally circle the full stops they find to begin with is an easy way into looking at this technique. Taking Heaney's 'Blackberry Picking' as a fantastic example, let's start with the first two lines. Students can pick out without too much difficulty that the lines *'Late August, given heavy rain and sun / For a full week, the blackberries would ripen'* continue from 'sun' to 'for' without a break. Ask them to consider the impact of this by writing out on the board *'Late August, given heavy rain and sun for a full week, the blackberries would ripen.'* What difference does the use of enjambment make? What does the snaking of the sentence across the two lines do for our understanding of the poem?

Even if they struggle initially to articulate the difference, simply by noticing that it **is** different they are beginning to feel their way towards an understanding of the use of the technique. You might want to nudge them to think about the fact that the opening lines are about waiting, about the time it takes for the much-anticipated blackberries to ripen, and allowing the sentence to drift from the first line to the second without a pause helps suggest that time is meandering on in an unhurried but inexorable manner – a sense which is perhaps missing from the example you have provided on the board for them.

Moving on to the section *'You ate that first one'* up until the first word of line eight, and your students will no doubt be able to spot the long length of this sentence and that the enjambment is spread across four lines. Ask them what the impact of this is. What is the poet describing? Why might it need a long sentence? By getting your students to think about the physical act of savouring a longed-for fruit they can imagine the poet rolling the enjoyment around his mouth like a long sentence, the sensation going on and on like the feeling of biting into the first blackberry and leaving a long-lasting impression on the tongue, just like the stain of the fruit.

Ask them to think about lines such as *'Round hayfields, cornfields and potato-drills'* until the end of the sentence. Again, the enjambment spreads this sentence over a number of lines, and nearly all students will spot this. Push them to think about why this is so significant. What action is taking place? Some students might want to act this out, or storyboard what is taking place so that they can fully appreciate the breadth of the actions that Heaney is covering. Nearly all students can see a link between the aching legs that *'trekked'* as the sentence plods on over a number of lines, like the children's feet going over *'hayfields, cornfields and potato-drills'*, but you can push more able or confident students to think about how memories are now piling up and spreading out in this slightly nostalgic section, just like the words in the sentence are spilling over from line to line. Remind them to consider pace, as it can be a common misconception that a series of short, abrupt sentences with monosyllabic words in them would have a faster pace than one long sentence with polysyllabic words. This long sentence, snaking through the mid-section of the poem with repeated use of enjambment, gives a pacey sense to Heaney's account and reflects the busyness and activity of this special time of year.

Sheers uses enjambment in a manner that is just as accessible to Key Stage 3 students, but in a slightly different way in his poem 'Mametz Wood'. The poem, which explores the uncovering of fallen soldiers from the First World War as farmers plough the battlefields nearly a century later, uses the technique to suggest not only the link between the past and the present but also to convey an impression to the reader of the field being ploughed. The opening lines *'For years afterwards the farmers found them – / the wasted young, turning up under their plough blades / as they tended the land back into itself'* has one sentence spread over three lines to create one complete stanza. By now your students will be familiar enough with the technique of enjambment to spot the device that Sheers has used, and you will be accustomed to pushing them from simply spotting the enjambment to thinking about the part it plays in our understanding of the poem. The sentence's length suggests something to us about time passing: there are *'years afterwards'* but farmers have still *'found them'*, giving us the impression that we are all linked to the past in the way the whole stanza is linked through one sentence.

By now your students will feel used to linking the poetic technique of enjambment with the themes and meaning of the poem. So you can set them a challenge to look at stanzas two and three, which they'll quickly note uses enjambment not only with continuous lines within the stanza but also bridging the two stanzas. Of course you'll be asking them why Sheers has made this choice, and as always it can help clarify the impact of the poet's choice by looking at the alternative. What would be the difference if he had one, much larger, second stanza? What is the effect of putting that stanza break somewhere else in the sentence? Does the fragmented structure linked by the enjambment suggest to the students that the men were as vulnerable when they fought as they are now, when their remains are being turned over, as the sentence links the past violence with the present action? Allow them to explore different and contrasting interpretations, and let them know that, although there needs to be a definite identification of the poetic technique, there can be a multitude of interpretations about **why** the poet or author has decided to use it. Exploring a number of different and even conflicting ideas can help students to think deeply about the authorial intention.

If you feel your students are ready to be pushed a little more, Sheers' poem provides another useful view of enjambment. Guide your students to think about what is physically happening in the poem – get them to consider how the scene is set. As they remember that, aside from it being the scene of a First World War battle, this is a field that is being ploughed, get them to look closely at the pattern on the page made through the poet's use of enjambment. More perceptive students will be able to make the link between the flow of the sentences across the lines and stanzas with the action of the plough as it moves across the field, turning and continuing on rather than finishing at the end of each row. It is always worth pushing the idea of how this furthers our understanding of the poem, and what it might suggest the poet is asking us to consider. As the poem shows the link again and again between the past and the present, it can easily be perceived that this unending pattern of enjambment reflected in the continuity of the ploughing motion contributes to the message that we can easily mix the past and the present, making us see the continuing horror of war.

Going forwards, allow your students to play around with how any poem being studied is set out on the page, to explore the use of enjambment and the effect it has. By showing alternatives – how the poem could have been if each sentence were a complete line, or if sentences were shortened – students can be helped to truly appreciate why the poets have made the choices they have.

Assonance

Assonance is likely to be a new term for your students as they begin Key Stage 3, but it can be illuminating for them to consider the impact it has on their appreciation of a text. Younger students are often open to experimenting verbally with a text and, with their willingness to speak a poem aloud or in a group, they have a great opportunity to really hear the repetition of any of the sounds they are making. Rather than seeing this as a 'words on the page' process, encourage them to read a poem aloud, rolling the sounds around their mouths and listening to any emphasis that seems to occur naturally or repetition that they can pick up on aurally. Before self-consciousness kicks in, get your students into the habit of thinking of assonance as something they hear rather than something they see, and then engage them in discussion and analysis of what effect these sounds might have.

To return to Seamus Heaney's 'Blackberry Picking', get students to read the poem aloud and listen to which vowel sounds seem to dominate. If they're unsure, get them to repeat the opening two lines and *'glossy purple clot'* and see how they can play with the sounds. The opening lines clearly have a preponderance of 'u' sounds in words like *'August . . . sun . . . full'*. Ask them to make the sound or repeat the words with emphasis as they read aloud. What does it evoke? Students will soon be able to hear the guttural longing of this vowel, reflecting the deep wish for blackberries to gather. The repeated 'o' sound in *'glossy'* and *'clot'* gives a roundness to the mouth that they'll be able to see if they watch each other pronounce the words, and students can then make the link between the mouth shape needed to annunciate this 'o' and the formation of the lips as ready for some sweet treat. As the poem progresses, get them to contrast this with repeated 'o' sounds in the poem's final two lines. Here we move away from the anticipatory roundedness of the assonance in the opening of the poem to a deeper sense of ponderousness and melancholy of *'rot . . . hoped . . . not'*. It is the same sound but this time used as a complete contrast, as the assonance tolls the doom not only of the rotting and wasted blackberries but the end of the innocence and hope of the narrator as he's faced with the realisation of life's disappointments.

'Mametz Wood' also offers you a great opportunity for exploring how the understanding of assonance can heighten student understanding of the poem. Ask them to look at a few words or a short phrase, such as *'like a wound working a foreign body to the surface'*. Pretty much everyone will feel confident about recognising the repeated use of the 'o' sound here, and, as always, you can give your class a chance to discuss what the impact of this choice is. What would be the effect if different vocabulary had been chosen? You might want students to think about the gaping sound that comes with the word *'wound'* so that we are imagining the land blasted apart during the military conflict and still bearing the scar. Also think about the physical impact of a wound on the body, again open like the consonant 'o' or the mouth as it forms the letter, or the way the conflict of 1914–1918 still echoes with us today, leaving a wound on the national consciousness. Further on, in the sixth stanza, the repetition of that 'o', as the poet explains that the remains of the soldiers have their jaws *'dropped open'*, shows your students mimicking the dropped-open jaws of the skeletons as they enunciate the words themselves. Sheers uses assonance as an illuminating way to connect the reader with what was found in the fields, and you can help your students see that as a technique. It isn't something just to spot and then move on from, but something to explore and consider so that students become used to wringing the meaning out of poems through their application of terminology.

Connotation

Connotation can sometimes seem an overly formal way for you to be asking the simple question 'What does x in the poem make the reader think about?', but we have found that equipping our students with this piece of vocabulary gives them a sense of validity when making connections in a poem which they aren't sure are 'right' or 'relevant'. From Year 7 your students can see that their written responses seem far more sophisticated when they are able to suggest that the mention of the dark cloud has a connotation of threat or danger, for instance, rather than merely stating the dark cloud makes them think of threat or danger. By seeing this as an essential tool in their arsenal of analytical devices, you will be ensuring that your class thinks about individual elements of vocabulary and explores what these make them think of. Consider what the impact of this will be on their understanding of a text or even the mood or atmosphere of a poem.

It is understandable that some teachers shy away from the term connotation because there can be a sense of the ephemeral or a difficulty in defining it. However, by straightforwardly explaining to your students that it refers to an association that a word evokes, beyond the literal meaning – such as 'safety' or 'warmth' for home – then they are likely to understand that the 'reason' a poem or a text makes them think of a particular idea or mood that isn't explicitly mentioned is because of the connotation of the author's particular vocabulary choices. Illuminating this idea to them also helps to provide the level of AO2 sophistication their writing needs to develop.

'Blackberry Picking' by Seamus Heaney is a poem saturated with connotations of childhood and the sense of growing up in rural Northern Ireland, and, as such, is a fantastic place to begin to explore this concept for your students. You can start before even looking at the poem by asking them what blackberry picking makes them think of. Among the responses about the painfulness of the thorns and the inevitable stains on clean clothes, students always talk about childhood, about summer and about being out of doors. Before they even realise it you've led them to see the connotations of blackberry picking, which are so important to understanding the deeper meanings of the poem. As you read it through, ask them to decide in which stage of life this poem is set (babyhood, childhood, adulthood etc.) and to pick out the specific words or phrases that refer to childhood in the poem. Apart from the poem clearly being in the past tense, they will be surprised to discover that nowhere in the poem does Heaney mention childhood directly, yet readers can immediately detect the connotations of childhood through indirect associations within the poem's vocabulary.

Help your students by picking out phrases such as *'It wasn't fair'* and *'You ate that first one'* which have such straightforward, almost mundane, vocabulary so they are able to see that even simple phrases can have such strong connotations. All children have, at some point, declared that *'it isn't fair'* and they'll be able to explore the connotations of that in the poem from the emotions they felt when they uttered the words. They will also be able to understand the frustration and baffled powerlessness in the face of the wrong that Heaney is suggesting is felt when the blackberries spoil. The link between the importance of 'firsts' in childhood, whether the first time they'll have experienced something or being the first to do something, is an idea you can guide your students to as they encounter lines such as *'You ate that first one'*. From there your students will again be able to see that Heaney gives strong connotations about childhood without specifically mentioning that period in life.

A really accessible phrase from the poem for you to begin to explore connotation would be *'rat-grey fungus'*. Either before or after reading the poem it can be a useful exercise for you to ask your students what each word in this phrase brings to mind. It is only a small step from thinking about how generally rats are seen as repulsive, diseased and repugnant for them to think about the connotations this is suggesting in the poem. Each word in the three-word phrase is loaded with bleak and depressing connotations, and this can help your students to explore how dark the end of the second stanza is as Heaney shows the reader that life can be a series of disappointments and upsets in spite of seemingly pleasant activities such as picking blackberries.

By asking your students to make a list of vocabulary from the poem with both pleasant and unpleasant associations, you'll have a great starting point for an exploration of the mood and atmosphere of the whole piece. Is Heaney suggesting to us that this is a happy experience or not? Although the narrative of the poem and the structure suggest to us that it is – with the emphasis on the summer, the sun and the communal act of gathering, especially as stanza one is so much longer than stanza two, when the blackberries rot – the exploration of the poem's vocabulary through the connotations it suggests gives a far more balanced representation. You can guide your students to look at phrases such as *'its flesh was sweet'*. Obviously the choice of *'sweet'* suggests happiness, but this is juxtaposed with the more sensual use of *'flesh'* to describe the fruit, which begins to bring connotations of decay and the end of innocence. The list of vocabulary with less than wholly pleasant associations in that first evocative stanza (heavy, rain, clot, red, hard, knot, flesh, blood, stains etc.) shows the importance to the reader of exploring the connotations of word choices. Most students can pick up on the idea that the poem is not presenting an idyllic and nostalgic view of childhood – the *'thorn pricks'* and the *'rat-grey fungus'* make that clear enough – but, by exploring the connotations of some of the more innocuous-seeming phrases and word choices, you can lead them to see why the poem has such a darkness to it.

'Mametz Wood' can also show your class that even innocuous choices of vocabulary can suggest far more than the surface seems to portray. The sparseness of the poem makes the connotations of each word seem even more significant, and you can help your students become confident in their exploration by simply highlighting on a copy of the poem any phrase or word you'd like them to provide connotations for before you begin any more formal analysis. *'Wasted young'* is a hugely powerful phrase, and for Key Stage 3 students the exploration of connotations about youth and how it can be exploited can make their understanding of the personal nature of the loss of life suffered in the battle so much more real for them. By asking your class what 'being young' is about, they'll make connections between their own sense of promise for the future, or ambition, or even sense of invincibility that the young soldiers who died in the battles must have shared with them. Connotations of being young will personalise the loss of life for them in a way that will deepen the sense of tragedy that the poem is trying to convey.

You can consider bringing to life the connotations in the poem by actually bringing the physical objects mentioned by Sheers into the classroom. Hand around a *'china plate'* or a *'broken bird's egg'* and ask your students how they feel. What do they associate them with? What are they like? They'll soon produce a word-bank of vocabulary about the objects that they'll then be able to transfer to writing about the soldiers' vulnerability, and truly understand the connotations of the china plate and the bird's egg that Sheers has tried to convey. The very nature of the physicality of the poet's imagery can provide your students with a tangible exploration of the connotations of the vocabulary. If you can procure a shattered bone or some old army boots, and ask them how these make them feel, you'll be providing them with a second-hand sense of what the farmers felt as they uncovered the grave. The connotations from young men being reduced to remnants that are churned up in the soil will help them understand the tribute that Sheers is paying to these soldiers.

 **Key Stage 4**

With the focus on the GCSE examination, and the swift pace of the course, it can be tempting to rush when studying poetry with Key Stage 4 students; concentrating more on the content of the poems than on the vocabulary needed for analysis, so that you know your pupils have 'done' all the poems on the syllabus and have time to revise them. While this is understandable – it is unlikely there's a teacher alive who hasn't felt the pressure just to push through the course content as time ticks away at lightning speed – it isn't the best approach for fostering an understanding of poetic techniques and will undermine the confidence of your students when they are faced with unseen poems in their examinations. Knowing particular poems well and knowing how to analyse any poem are two quite separate skills, and it is the latter that we should all be doing our best to promote in our classrooms.

Ensure, then, that you spend time exploring not just the techniques in the poems they'll be examined on but also how these devices are used more generally. By exploring, for example, pathetic fallacy in 'Porphyria's Lover' by Robert Browning and then looking at Lennox's speech in Act 2, Scene 3 of *Macbeth*, students will gain a far deeper understanding of the term and how it can be applied across literature. A quick look at the section below will enable them to see this as a frequently used device and give them the confidence to apply the term 'pathetic fallacy' when they see it elsewhere:

> *The night has been unruly: where we lay,*
> *Our chimneys were blown down; and, as they say,*
> *Lamentings heard i' the air; strange screams of death,*
> *And prophesying with accents terrible*
> *Of dire combustion and confused events*
> *New hatch'd to the woeful time: the obscure bird*
> *Clamour'd the livelong night: some say, the earth*
> *Was feverous and did shake.* (Act 2, Scene 3, lines 49–56)
> (Oxford: Oxford University Press, 2009)

Pathetic fallacy

Pathetic fallacy is a great place for you to start with your students, who will no doubt be familiar with the idea of personification and will only need a little more information to feel comfortable with this new term. Clearly pathetic fallacy is a type of personification, but the emphasis is on the idea of attributing human emotions or qualities to objects in nature, and the actions or emotions of characters will be reflected in the natural world around them. You might wish to spend some time making the difference between the two terms clear for your students; emphasising that they are very much 'related' to each other, giving examples of both techniques and then asking your class to decide which is pathetic fallacy and which a more straightforward personification (to push very able students it could be worth throwing in a few examples of zoomorphism and anthropomorphism, too).

To begin with, let's take a look at 'Porphyria's Lover', which appears on many exam board syllabi at GCSE and has the power to shock and surprise students who might initially be put off by the length and seemingly antiquated nature of the poem.

> *The rain set early in tonight,*
> *The sullen wind was soon awake,*
> *It tore the elm-tops down for spite,*
> *And did its worst to vex the lake:*

These first lines are a perfect example of pathetic fallacy, and asking your students to underline or highlight anything that relates to the natural world and the emotions being attributed to it is an easy and accessible way into the poem. The poem's next line, *'I listened with heart fit to break'*, is a clear signal to the reader that it is no coincidence there is rain and wind, and the emotions being described are *'sullen'*, *'spite'* and the power to *'vex'*. This is a good starting point, but you'll want to move your students quickly beyond the ability to spot the example of pathetic fallacy to understanding why it is so important. Ask them why Browning has done this. What is the signal to the reader about both the mood of the poem and the character of the narrator? Do we feel this poem is likely to have a happy mood? And, if not, why not?

After reading the entire poem, revisit this opening and ask your students to rethink it. If Browning shows the natural world to be malevolent without any particular cause and without reason, just a destructive and powerful force, what is he telling us about the narrator killing Porphyria? It can be tempting to look for a definite reason as to why he strangled her, but you need to remind your students that Browning isn't providing us with any. We can look for hints, through Porphyria's *'soiled gloves'* suggesting a moral laxity, or that she's arrived at the cottage from *'to-night's gay feast'*, which might indicate some duplicity in her actions, but the narrator is unreliable – after all, he is convinced his victim *'felt no pain'* as he brutally strangled her! So maybe, as readers, we should be looking at the poem's use of pathetic fallacy for the 'reason' it happened: sometimes a person's mood or character can be as destructive and turbulent as the weather, without there being any more reason to it than the day being stormy. Browning wants us to see how random and shocking the events are, and by his use of pathetic fallacy there's a scene set from the very first line of darkness, misery and upset.

Again, don't feel you're wasting time during discussions if you bring in other texts to illustrate the use of pathetic fallacy. There are many other examples in the poetry anthologies students study for their examinations and in the fiction texts that they frequently encounter. Remind them of the oppressive weather and the violent storm in the section of *Lord of the Flies* that leads to Simon's death, or the first appearance of Mr Hyde in *The Strange Case of Dr Jekyll and Mr Hyde* as the darkness of the city is mirrored in the anonymity of the character and the blackness of his actions. By showing the broadness of examples across literary texts they're familiar with, you'll be allowing your students to feel they are fully in command of the term.

Epizeuxis

This is the sort of term that might initially make your students cringe back doubtfully, but it is actually incredibly useful; not only will it add a sophisticated polish to their work, but repetition in texts is often an easy technique to spot and a very important one to analyse. A cynic might suggest that simply using the word repetition would suffice, but where's the fun in that? As a teacher you clearly want to increase the vocabulary of your students, and epizeuxis is a great example of this. It is easy to spot a word being used again and again in quick succession, and many students will instinctively suggest that this is done 'for emphasis' but won't push the idea further. Your job will be to move them beyond spotting the technique and ensuring they are being clear in their responses about what exactly is being emphasised and how the vehemence is being employed for meaning.

As always, with one eye on the mark scheme of the GCSE examinations, this technique is likely to crop up not only in literary texts but in non-fiction, particularly in speeches, so it really is worth a thorough exploration. Again, poetry is a great place to begin. Let's take Alfred, Lord Tennyson's 'The Charge of the Light Brigade' as our first example. The opening stanza is arresting in its use of epizeuxis:

> *Half a league, half a league,*
>   *Half a league onward,*
> *All in the valley of Death*
>   *Rode the six hundred.*
> *"Forward, the Light Brigade!*
> *"Charge for the guns!" he said:*
> *Into the valley of Death*
>   *Rode the six hundred.*

It is a clear and easy example to spot, and this will obviously be a great opportunity for you to ensure that everyone in the room is happy with the definition of epizeuxis and knows what they are looking for. Unlike at Key Stage 3, students by Key Stage 4 can sometimes feel a little overwhelmed when they encounter new vocabulary in English, and this is a great opportunity to show them that there is nothing to be frightened of. 'The Charge of the Light Brigade' should help with this, and by now your students will be familiar with finding an example of a technique and immediately beginning to consider why it has been used and its impact.

As contextual ideas are so important at Key Stage 4 you'll have wanted to provide some background to the poem so your students are aware of the events of the battle and how the army would have appeared at the time. Although this might not immediately seem to be connected to the idea of epizeuxis, by being able to link techniques in the poem to the context surrounding the poem your students will be able to access far higher marks in examinations. Establish with them that the soldiers involved were the cavalry and that Tennyson was trying to create a sense of patriotic fervour in England when he wrote the poem. These ideas are completely intertwined with the use of epizeuxis.

Let's consider the opening two lines. Clearly you'll expect your students to see that the phrase *'half a league'* has been used three times. Someone in the class will probably suggest that this has been done for emphasis. But now you'll want to swiftly move on to analysing what the emphasis is. Ask them to think back to the context and how these men were approaching the enemy. The epizeuxis immediately creates a thundering rhythm which evokes elements of the battle, whether it is the pounding of the horses' hooves, the sound of military drums, or even the hammering hearts in the shuddering chests of the nervous cavalry officers as they approached the enemy – and this is immediately linked to that vital mention of context.

Moving further into the poem, the repetition of *'the six hundred'*, which appears in line four as well as the final line of each stanza, also provides a challenge for students to link to context. Why are they constantly being referenced? They aren't named and, aside from the mention of *'he said'*, they are consistently seen as a mass of men rather than individuals, which is emphasised through the epizeuxis. Challenge your students to think why this is, and again link them back to the context. Tennyson was at the absolute height of his fame and popularity when the poem was written, and was known for writing pieces which marked important occasions. So you can prompt them to think about the power he had over how the population – and even posterity – would remember these men; the continual use of *'the six hundred'* reminds the reader that these were men, and yet they acted as one in the face of appalling danger and terrible slaughter because *'someone had blundered'*. Remind your students that this sense of *'the six hundred'* is reinforcing the patriotic sense that every last man was brave and rode to their death without hesitation. You can also link this to the sense of what 'being British' meant at the time, the patriotic fervour and almost jingoistic pride in the British army.

Tennyson continues with this throughout the poem. *'Cannon to the right of them / Cannon to the left of them / Cannon in front of them'* shows yet more epizeuxis, and your students will want to explore how this has created the sense of the men being relentlessly in danger and peril, and the inevitability of their fate as *'Into the jaws of death, / Into the mouth of Hell'* they rode. The graphic nature of the poem, emphasised through Tennyson's use of epizeuxis, combines with insight into the national psyche at the time and will provide your students with a fantastic way to link AO2 and AO3 in a sophisticated manner.

Epizeuxis is also of crucial importance in 'Porphyria's Lover', where you again have an opportunity to stretch your students beyond seeing it as a device 'for emphasis'. At the climax of the poem's action the narrator rather strikingly declares that Porphyria in that *'moment was mine, mine'*. Your students will quickly spot this use of the device and, again, you'll be able to push them to seeing that there is very much a climatic sense to this, with an urgent sense of sexual undertone as the narrator seems to finally feel fulfilled in the relationship. There's also an echo of the technique as the narrator seems to justify his acts to himself as he suggests *'No pain felt she; / I am quite sure she felt no pain'*, with the emphasis on this epizeuxis being made all the more plain for successive lines of the poem ending in the same adjective. Students will quickly be able to detect the sense that not only is this a signal of the narrator's delusion but also a suggestion of his muttering to himself following the act, further showing madness.

 Key Stage 5

By the time your students reach Key Stage 5 they should already have a wide range of terminology to draw on in order to identify features of texts and discuss their purpose and significance. However, with studying English at a higher level comes exposure to more complex texts, particularly from earlier periods where writers are using grammatical features that your students may well not have come across. It is essential that they can define and explain these more obscure turns of phrase, figures of speech or structural features, as this is a key success criterion at A Level as part of AO2. Helping students to widen their vocabulary of terminology to a more sophisticated level also starts to bridge the gap between secondary and higher education, as this will enable them to access more complex ideas and concepts they will come across in critical material.

Some of the terms we have defined in the table at the beginning of the chapter are quite obscure and so you may be coming to them for the first time, along with your students. Don't worry if there are terms you feel insecure in using or are struggling to identify in texts. There is no need for you to teach all of the devices we have listed and it doesn't matter if you can't come up with a definitive list of literary devices in every text you are teaching. Focusing on two or three interesting uses of terminology that you do feel confident discussing will provide students with more than enough on which to hinge their own analyses. Further to this, to make everyone's lives easier, we are firm believers in the philosophy that you only need to teach students the terminology they need to know in order to appreciate the texts they are studying. We would not recommend giving out exhaustive lists of complex terminology for students to learn as this often causes more confusion than clarity. Knowing a few relevant terms well is the most important thing.

A pitfall to avoid when teaching more challenging terms at this level is the tendency for students to rote-learn the terms in isolation and then not be able to apply them to the texts. They will need to be able to identify and explain the terms, thinking about their effect; identification is not enough, and students need to be fully secure in what these devices are actually doing within the texts, otherwise there is little point in them using the terminology at all. We would encourage you not to test students on their knowledge of the terminology outside of the context of their texts. If you want to check they have learned and understood a good pool of literary devices to draw on in their writing, then we would recommend providing quotations for students to match with a term in order to show their knowledge in practice, rather than just asking them to define what the term means.

To put the use of complex literary terminology into practice for Key Stage 5 we are going to look at two more commonly used devices – synaesthesia and metonymy – through analysis of the poems 'Goblin Market' by Christina Rossetti and 'Ode to a Nightingale' by John Keats. We find that, to root students in these terms, it is best to start with poetry; when they feel more confident in identifying and understanding these devices in shorter, more tightly constructed texts they tend to make the leap to novel and non-fiction analysis more easily.

Synaesthesia

Synaesthesia is one of the easier complex terms to understand as it is very straightforward to identify.

First of all, let's look at the use of synaesthesia in this extract from 'Goblin Market':

Morning and evening
Maids heard the goblins cry:
"Come buy our orchard fruits,
Come buy, come buy:
Apples and quinces,
Lemons and oranges,
Plump unpeck'd cherries,
Melons and raspberries,
Bloom-down-cheek'd peaches,
Swart-headed mulberries,
Wild free-born cranberries,
Crab-apples, dewberries,
Pine-apples, blackberries,
Apricots, strawberries;—
All ripe together
In summer weather,—
Morns that pass by,
Fair eves that fly;
Come buy, come buy:
Our grapes fresh from the vine,
Pomegranates full and fine,
Dates and sharp bullaces,
Rare pears and greengages,
Damsons and bilberries,

Taste them and try:
Currants and gooseberries,
Bright-fire-like barberries,
Figs to fill your mouth,
Citrons from the South,
Sweet to tongue and sound to eye;
Come buy, come buy."

This section is typical of the poem in its use of multi-sensory imagery to overwhelm the reader with a thrilling sense of pleasure. On the surface the synaesthesia is being used here to create a vivid picture of the abundance of the fruits these goblins have to sell, and allow the reader to smell, see and touch them through the choice of words: *'bloom-down-cheek'd peaches'*, *'bright-fire-like barberries'* and *'figs to fill your mouth'* are all excellent examples of this. The effect of the synaesthesia is aided by the use of alliteration and onomatopoeia, heightening the feel of sensory overload the language creates. Rossetti is using synaesthesia to emphasise the huge choice the goblins offer, and, through this choice, temptation. This allows readers to understand how Laura in the poem is so overwhelmed by the goblins, as they too are overwhelmed by the assault on their senses that Rossetti's language provides.

At Key Stage 5, your students will be expected to start to draw on critical interpretations to add to their own analysis of texts, and the synaesthesia here is a perfect opportunity to look at feminist criticism. The sensuality of the poem and the particular use of touching with the mouth – *'she suck'd and suck'd and suck'd some more'* – have led to many critics discussing the goblins and their fruit as being representative of sexual temptation. *'Sweet tooth'd'* Laura becomes a fallen woman, who wastes away after succumbing to the temptation of the goblin men and needs to be saved by the Christ-figure of her sister. The synaesthesia that features in the language throughout the poem, presenting the body and its sensations at the forefront of the reading experience, allows Rossetti to explore the physical, sensual desires of the body without making any explicit reference to sex. Her use of the metaphor of forbidden fruit for sexual desire was so subtle to a Victorian audience that for many years it was considered nothing more than a fairytale poem for children, and this is an interesting way into exploring how many women writers in the nineteenth century were forced to cloak their true feelings in metaphor in order to allow their voices to be heard.

Synaesthesia is therefore vital to understanding and analysing 'Goblin Market', and it also features in Keat's 'Ode to a Nightingale':

O, for a draught of vintage! that hath been
Cool'd a long age in the deep-delved earth,
Tasting of Flora and the country green,
Dance, and Provençal song, and sunburnt mirth!
O for a beaker full of the warm South,
Full of the true, the blushful Hippocrene,

With beaded bubbles winking at the brim,
And purple-stained mouth;
That I might drink, and leave the world unseen,
And with thee fade away into the forest dim:

This poem, which explores the speaker's desire to escape the cares of the world on the wings of a nightingale, uses synaesthesia as a means to demonstrate the richness of life and the happiness it can offer. The stanza above is describing the wish of the speaker to be transported by alcohol into the bliss of *'country green'* and the *'warm South'*, giving a vivid visual image of shaded green lanes as well as evoking the warmth of the sun on the skin. Sound is also suggested through the *'Provençal song'* and taste through the *'beaded bubbles'* and *'purple-stained mouth'*. This truly multi-sensory stanza allows the reader to be transported with the speaker to a halcyon world of warmth, light and mirth that will be a flight from the *'the weariness, the fever and the fret'* of life. The synaesthesia is so effective here because it provides an immersive experience and adds to the idea of escape that the poem explores through the speaker's longing to fly with the nightingale away from the cares of the world.

Contextual links worth making are to the use of opiates and other recreational drugs at this time in history, and the interest in the late eighteenth and early nineteenth centuries in the subliminal mind. It is interesting that while the speaker imagines himself to be in an impaired state, either through drugs or alcohol, he also describes his projected experiences through highly synaesthetic language, perhaps suggesting a belief that humans can only fully experience the fullness of life through artificial means.

As can be seen from these examples, synaesthesia is a wonderful example of a complex literary device from which students can build thoughtful and useful analyses that add much to their understanding of the text. Rather than just talking vaguely about the use of senses, being able to talk in detail about the purpose and effect of multi-sensory imagery and how this links clearly to the themes of the poem itself will take their analysis in a much more interesting and sophisticated direction. Do encourage your students to push their analysis as far as they can take it, using these more advanced terms to explore the wider themes and contextual significance of the text.

Metonymy

Metonymy is commonly used in texts to allow readers to make a series of connections to something through using a word that relates either materially or conceptually to it. Rather than using a specific simile or metaphor, metonymy allows readers to bring their own meanings to the text by making the implied connection themselves through word association. We'll look at an example from Keats' 'Ode to a Nightingale' to show it in practice.

O, for a draught of vintage! that hath been
Cool'd a long age in the deep-delved earth,
Tasting of Flora and the country green,
Dance, and Provençal song, and sunburnt mirth!

Here Keats replaces the word 'wine' with *'vintage'*, which is an interesting use of metonymy. The drinking of wine is connoted with joy and ease, leading its drinker to a state of bliss. The use of synaesthesia, as discussed above, makes this description of inebriation intensely romantic and attractive, with the idea of the warm sun, the green leaves and the sound of the music expressed through synaesthetic imagery. However, why does Keats deliberately not refer to wine as wine? Why does he use the word *'vintage'* instead? What connotations is he wishing the reader to draw? First, vintage implies age and quality – a wine that has been waiting for the right opportunity to be drunk. This could be suggesting that the speaker is not some wayward wastrel, a drunkard who is wont to spend his free time drinking whatever alcohol he can lay his hands on to forget the dismal reality of his existence. No, he is referring to a very special bottle of wine, one that is of excellent quality, made of the best ingredients, that has been saved and treasured, and so embodies all that is wondrous about summer. This speaker is therefore not someone who wants to get drunk and forget the world, but someone who wants to have a heightened appreciation of it. He wants to experience what the nightingale experiences, and one way he can think to do this is by drinking something of the finest quality which will contain the richness and superiority of flavour needed to allow him to enter into the nightingale's existence.

It would be easy for students to overlook the use of the word *'vintage'* entirely here, thinking it to be unimportant. By understanding the term metonymy and looking out for it, therefore, seemingly insignificant word changes such as *'vintage'* for 'wine' can offer a window into a more interesting and sophisticated interpretation of the poem. At A Level, when studying texts that have been analysed to death and have quite standardised 'correct' interpretations, students can struggle with finding something interesting to say or to have their own take on the text. Metonymy and its close relative synecdoche can offer the eagle-eyed reader a way to make a subtle and much more individual point that will take their analysis to a more exciting and vibrant level.

SUGGESTED LESSON PLAN

This activity can be adapted for any level of student and the table of definitions can be simplified for different Key Stages, or clues given to assist students. Any text can be used for the final part of the lesson, either covering set poems from GCSE anthologies or picking a text that is suitable for the age group intended.

Equipment needed:
Multiple sets of the terminology, definitions, and examples
Photocopies of chosen extract/text

L/O: To extend and cement the use of ambitious vocabulary

This lesson is designed to be lively and to require some space to make it work. Do not be afraid to push the desks back and to use the floor, and allow your students time to think, work in a team and really get to grips with the puzzle you have set them. Depending on how many of the definitions you use, this activity could take a significant amount of time. However, by making the activity competitive (first group to finish, group to get most correct within 15 minutes, group to come up with the best examples on their own etc.) the lesson remains engaging and fun; students encountering some new vocabulary will be undaunted and relish the challenge of how and when to use it. Do not be afraid to challenge your students even if this creates a noisy but focused atmosphere. This lesson can also be easily adapted using just a few of the examples of terminology as a starter or revision activity.

Starter (5–10 minutes)

Split the class into small groups of no more than four people. For a task like this, ensuring there is a mix of abilities in each group can be useful, or the task can be tailored so that different groups have a differentiated challenge later.

Each group should be given a large piece of blank paper and allocated five minutes to come up with as many different examples of vocabulary they can when analysing poetic and literary techniques. After five minutes each group should join with another group to pool their ideas, adding in another colour any other suggestions they've gleaned from the second group. On returning to their original small group they can then spend a few minutes trying to add definitions to their terminology and discussing where they have seen examples in literature they've read.

Main (35 minutes)

Before the lesson, print out the table below, one for each group. Then cut each table out (as a tip, if you'd like to reuse this resource, print each table on different colours so the sets don't get mixed up!) and challenge the students to put them together.

Although it can be hard to stand back, give your students time and space to work on the task. There can be a variety of different approaches – either asking people to first line up the definitions and terms and then adding in the quotations, or taking a completely hands-off approach by giving students the pieces and simply letting them work out what needs to be done. It can be useful to set a deadline for every group to complete the task, or simply stop when the first group has matched all the elements for each definition.

Five minutes before the end of the task ask your students to stop (and possibly have one final check of their work!) and step away from their table. Then ask each group to swap, ready to check the work of their peers. Arm each group with some post-it notes so they can highlight which answers are not completely correct. You can either simply show them the table or read out the answers, and, depending on how much of a spirit of competitiveness you like to foster, award points for fully correct or partially correct answers. Then invite students to return to their original table and see how they did.

In the group, the students should then correct any mistakes they've made (and be assured that, if there are challenging definitions and examples for them, there will be mistakes for all students) and make a note of any definitions or terminology that were problematic.

Plenary (5–10 minutes)

This is a brilliant opportunity for consolidation of learning. Students should highlight the terminology they are unsure of – either singly, in pairs or in a group – and try again to match them with the correct definition and example. After doing this, in pairs, they should quiz each other on the terminology to ensure they are now able to correctly define the vocabulary being used. It can also be useful as a teacher-led activity here if the examples are read out and students are asked to identify the example of terminology being used.

Differentiation

This activity is very easy to adapt to the needs of students, so that those who require more support can be pushed to achieve while the most able are still being sufficiently challenged. By adding in some more simple terminology, such as verbs or determiners, students who are not confident to recognise more complex ideas such as parallelism can still be challenged and consolidate their knowledge. Adaptation of the examples, so that sibilance is made more apparent, is a way to scaffold information so that the same task is accessible to different abilities. For example:

*S*weet dream*s*, form a *s*hade
O'er my lovely infant*s* head.
*S*weet dream*s* of plea*s*ant *s*tream*s*
By happy *s*ilent moony beam*s*
*S*weet *s*leep with *s*oft down.

Even keeping the terminology and the example together can make the definitions easier to decipher for students who are not feeling confident.

Those who require more challenging work can be asked to come up with a definition for the terminology, based on their past knowledge and the example they have been given. They can also be stretched to provide an example from literature that they know or create one themselves. Missing out any part of the three elements will provide a more challenging task, but those who are familiar with the terminology can be pushed to apply their knowledge by then suggesting what the effect on the reader is from each of the examples they are given. For example, using the sibilance quotation again, a very competent student would be able to suggest that the repetition of the 's' sound in the extract could evoke the idea of a baby being shushed to sleep with a lullaby, through the softness of the consonant sound. By allowing them to move beyond defining to understanding and application, those who require more challenge in their work will be able to see why a command of these terms is so important.

Provision of more advanced vocabulary – such as syllogism, metonym and synecdoche – could also be employed for those students who are most able, and they can be tasked with providing their own examples, possibly after being presented with one first.

 Additional ideas

Including literary terminology in essay writing

Students can sometimes struggle when making the leap from talking about literary devices to writing about them. It can be difficult to make using literary devices a natural part of a discussion and sometimes students can fall into the trap of shoehorning in references or making simplistic observations about the existence of devices without actually explaining what meaning they bring to the text.

We use a simple formula to help our students to understand how to effectively write essays using literary devices, and it works as follows:

Identification of device + quotation + explanation of meaning + link to entire text

This formula follows the P-E-E-L method that many teachers use to teach analytical paragraphing (point, evidence, explanation, link) in some form or another. There are many acronyms out there for this structure and you will no doubt have your own that you use in your classroom. Modelled in practice, the technique looks like this:

Keats uses metonymy in 'Ode to a Nightingale' when he refers to wine as 'vintage' in the first line of stanza two: 'O, for a draught of vintage! that hath been / Cool'd a long age in the deep-delved earth.' The metonymic use of 'vintage' allows the reader to make connections of quality and preciousness to the wine the speaker wishes to drink in order to transport himself to the same plane as the nightingale he so admires. Rather than the associations of drunkenness or oblivion that might come more naturally with the use of the word 'wine', 'vintage' allows the reader to understand that Keats' speaker wishes to drink something carefully chosen, something that has been allowed to rest until it has reached its zenith of taste, offering an intensive rather than deadening sensual experience. This use of metonymy to connote the idea of heady perfection therefore links to the overall meaning of the poem, which is about the speaker wishing to enter into the free and 'light-winged' existence of the nightingale, a state of bliss he uses the poem as a musing on how to reach.

As can be seen here, there is quite a lot students can say about small sections of text. Often this focused and small-scale approach to analysis is more successful than trying to encompass the whole text in an essay, which tends to produce vague and poorly evidenced responses.

What you will want students to avoid are simplistic references to literary devices along the lines of:

The poet uses enjambment to make the reader read on.
The use of alliteration in line three makes the words stand out.

These types of comments are quite usual, particularly from Key Stage 3 students who want to show they know literary terminology but can't really find much of use to say about what the grammatical devices are actually doing within the text. As we all know, these sorts of sentences are incredibly frustrating to read and it is in all of our best interests to nip them in the bud as soon as possible. To encourage fully evidenced and explained answers right from the start when you begin to teach your students how to analyse texts using literary terminology, you might find it helpful to use a scaffolded approach to remind them of what to include. For example:

In line three there is an interesting use of alliteration. This is shown through the use of the words _____. The effect of this alliteration is to _____ which links to the overall meaning of the poem by _____ _____.

Giving this sort of scaffold to students who are struggling doesn't give them the answers, but merely nudges them towards developing their answers more fully. As they become more confident, the scaffold can be removed and students should then be able to reproduce this structure instinctively on their own.

Summing up

We hope that this chapter has showed how fulfilling it can be for students to be able to grapple with more complex literary devices and apply them to their understanding of texts. Terminology isn't just there to tick boxes for exam boards; it is a vital way for students to be able to articulate and legitimise their ideas, and also extend their analyses to a more sophisticated point than they can do without it. We hope our examples of analysis in practice have given you some practical ideas to use in the classroom, and that you'll soon be on your way to developing increased confidence with literary terminology in your students.

7 Activity A–Z

In this chapter we have come up with a variety of fun activities you can use to more fully incorporate grammar into your classrooms, using an A–Z format. Most can be used for any of the areas of grammar the book covers and can be adapted to function as short starter tasks or longer foci of the lesson, depending on your preference.

All change is a great way to liven up a lesson that involves a lot of quiet writing work. While students are working, shouting 'all change' from the front is the signal for them to stop writing, read over what they have written, and then consciously try to rewrite what they've just done in a completely different style, using their knowledge of grammatical structures to make relevant changes. Can they change a romance into a horror story?

Blank-out works really well to show students the function of particular features of grammar. By taking a section of text and blanking out all of the determiners, pronouns, nouns etc. – whatever you wish to focus on – students can then clearly see how the text is affected by their removal and understand more fully what that feature of grammar does within a sentence. This can also be used as a fun revision activity by giving students quotations they should be memorising with key words blanked out – and seeing if they can fill in the blanks without checking!

Consequences is a game you will no doubt already be familiar with, but, to give it a grammatical twist, try asking students to include a different grammatical feature on every turn for some additional challenge.

Die are a great tool for fun grammar games – rolling the dice and having students find the corresponding number of a particular grammatical feature in a text is a lively way to start a lesson and ensure students actually know how to identify the grammar feature they're supposed to be looking for.

Editor works well at increasing students' confidence in their own creative writing. Show them an extract from a published text and ask them to have a go at playing around with the grammar and punctuation to improve on it. They might be surprised at what they can do to make it even better.

Finger pointing is a great activity to use when looking at pronouns in a text, particularly Shakespeare. Have students say key lines and point at themselves or their partner at the appropriate moment in the speech, and use this activity as a starting point to discuss how pronouns are used for emphasis or meaning. This works especially well as a starter activity to help students access more complicated sections of texts.

Getting to know you is a game that works well with nouns and verbs in particular – students have to move around the room, describing themselves to one another only using words that perform a grammatical function you dictate. So if they can only use abstract nouns they will have to say things like 'Hello, I am enthusiasm and generosity, who are you?', or, if verbs, they will have to say 'Hello, I am running and swimming, who are you?' This is an active way to remind students of what particular grammatical features are before using them in an analysis activity.

Homophone game is a firm favourite with our students. They are tasked to think of a homophone, for example 'witch' and 'which', and then come up with a sentence which leads the audience to them without mentioning the actual homophone, such as 'I can't decide between two evil, magic women who I should pick'. The first person to get the answer and correctly show knowledge of the homophones gets to read the next one.

I-Spy can be given a grammatical twist by a word being chosen in a section of text and students having to guess which one it is by asking questions that contain grammatical definitions, such as 'is it in a compound sentence?' You can also play this in a more complex way by making students explain why the word is grammatically significant before they can be declared the winner. This works well as a fun starter for grammar revision or as a way into an unseen text.

Judge and jury is an interactive game that works particularly well as a smaller group activity. Give each group an extract of text and appoint one of them as the judge, one as the defence, one as the prosecutor, and one or two as the jury, depending on the group size. Each group needs to be given a grammatical focus to explore in their text – punctuation, use of nouns, use of verbs etc. The defence needs to argue for why the extract shows an excellent use of that feature, while the prosecutor has to argue why it is not a good use of the feature. The judge has to lead the discussion by asking appropriate questions, and the jury must decide whose argument is the most convincing. The activity can be differentiated by giving less-confident students the role of the jury and more confident ones the roles of the prosecutor and defence. This could also be expanded to become a whole-class activity if the defence and prosecution consist of teams rather than just one person.

Knock, Knock: similar to Getting to Know You, this exploits the familiar Knock, Knock joke format and works well in pairs. Students decide which grammatical feature they are, such as a determiner or a possessive pronoun, and their partner asks, 'Knock, Knock, who's there?' They then need to give an example of their word type or describe what it does in a sentence. The person in the pair who guesses with the fewest clues wins.

Line up is a fun and active way to show students how grammar works in practice – we particularly like using this with punctuation. Have students line up at the front of the room, each holding up a piece of paper with a word written on it that, when students are all assembled together with their words, helps form a sentence. Then have several students representing different punctuation marks and ask the class to decide who belongs in the sentence and where, moving people around as necessary. Seeing a sentence so visually like this can often make students who are struggling finally have their 'a-ha!' moment.

Mystery box is another good way to refresh knowledge of grammatical terms before using them practically in a lesson. Students can each have a sheet of paper, which they divide into four. They then draw a small picture of their favourite things, one thing in each of the four boxes, on the sheet of paper. Students then have to share their mystery box with a partner, who has to name each of the four objects using the lesson's chosen grammatical focus. So if it is abstract nouns, they have to think of a concept to describe the thing rather than using a concrete noun to literally describe it. This can present quite a difficult challenge and also remind students of the importance of connotation as they bring their own interpretations to the drawn objects.

Name that feature! is a fun guessing game to start a lesson. Show students a series of quotations on the board and ask them to identify a reason why the grammar being used is interesting – with the most insightful idea winning.

Opposites is a great way to get students to look at texts from a different perspective. We particularly like using this with punctuation. Requesting students to swap or take away punctuation marks – asking 'what if this wasn't here?' rather than what an existing punctuation mark is doing – can help them to see more clearly what its function is. This technique can also work for looking at adjectives, pronouns and determiners.

Pictionary is a brilliant way to revise at the end of a unit of work on a text. To give students a real analytical challenge, accompany each image to be drawn with a grammar-based question. For example, with *Lord of the Flies* the picture could be a conch and the question could be 'which abstract nouns does the concrete noun of "conch" represent?'

Queen's English is a fun game to allow students to experiment with grammar choices and sentence structure in their creative writing. Getting them to rewrite sentences as if the Queen were saying them can get them thinking about formal structures and more challenging concepts, such as the subjunctive and modal verbs. They can also enjoy reading them out loud in their best Queen accent!

Reducing texts down to solely nouns or verbs can be a great way for students to see the important elements of a story and summarise complex events. This works especially well with Shakespeare but can be a useful tool for any text at any level.

Slow writing is a fantastic way to allow students to think through their language choices and edit their work. Students leave a line free when they write an initial piece of creative writing, before going back with a different coloured pen and rewriting what they've written on the spare line underneath, this time restructuring and replacing words or punctuation to create a more successful piece. This can be very structured by requiring students to focus on a particular area of grammar, such as punctuation or adjectives, or can be left more open for students to use their entire knowledge base to improve their work.

Time trial is an activity that can work with any number of topics. Asking students to identify as many particular grammar features in a text as quickly as possible, with a prize for the winner, is a fantastic way to get a lesson started with a bang.

Unique or duplicate? Each student writes a sentence that they read out to the rest of the class. In it they decide on one grammatical feature that they will include, such as concrete nouns or adjectives. They can then either include one or two examples in their sentence. The trick for the rest of the class is to decide when they hear what the feature is, whether it appears more than once in the sentence or whether the example is unique. Extra points if they can repeat what the example of the feature was.

Verb volleyball is a great game for a lesson that needs livening up, or for students who need to let off some steam before getting down to some concentrated writing. Much like the real game, the idea is to keep the sentence 'in the air' with the ball by not pausing or allowing the momentum to drop. The class is given the start of a sentence, such as 'I went walking...' and the teacher throws a (soft!) ball to the person who speaks next. The next person needs to come up with a synonym verb, such as 'strolling' or 'hiking', and then bats away the ball to the next respondent. The game continues until someone can't keep going with the sentence before they have to nudge the ball on.

Washing line: ask your students to write down examples of grammar in their texts on cue card sized pieces of paper and hang them up on a washing line across the classroom ceiling. Finding interesting examples of nouns or verbs from the text can be great for this activity, which also functions as a fantastic revision tool for quotation memorisation.

X-ray eyes: this can be an especially useful activity for helping students gain confidence with unseen texts. Give students a section of a text they don't know and ask them to use 'x-ray eyes' to find as many interesting grammatical features as they can, or ask them to focus on finding a specific grammatical feature – whatever you prefer. The key with this activity is making sure students do not read any of the whole text first – they are simply to x-ray it to find what they are looking for, before going back and reading the whole text for meaning. By looking for items in the text before knowing what the text is about, students are often more alive to spotting unusual or interesting features as they are not distracted by making sense of it. This can also work for known texts if you want students to focus on finding unusual features in a well-known extract that they may be overlooking.

You decide is a fantastic way for students to solidify sentence types. Quickly write on separate pieces of paper 'Simple', 'Complex', 'Compound' and 'Nonsense' and stick one on each wall. Ask all your students to stand in the middle of the room and you begin to tell a story, one sentence at time, using a mix of simple, complex, compound and nonsense sentences. As you read each sentence they go and stand under the sign they've decided the sentence type is. We find that displaying the sentences on the board can help consolidate our students' learning as we do this, with some students needing to see the sentence before deciding on what type it is. Spot-checking why someone has chosen the sign they've picked can stop there being too much 'follow the most able' during this activity!

Zap is a variation on the popular drama game, and also begins in a circle. Give the students a word type, such as a noun, and as they go around in the circle they need to shout out in turn a word that is a noun. After a few goes you shout 'Zap!' and change the word type. If you want to make this more challenging be *really* specific, selecting abstract nouns rather than just nouns, or single pronouns rather than pronouns. See how long the class can go without making a mistake. We have found that even Key Stage 5 students can become very competitive during these sessions.

Bibliography

Novels
Austen, Jane, *Emma* (Ware: Wordsworth Classics, 2007)
— *Pride and Prejudice* (London: Penguin, 2003)
Boyne, John, *The Boy in the Striped Pyjamas* (Oxford: David Fickling Books, 2006)
Brontë, Charlotte, *Jane Eyre* (London: Penguin, 2006)
Brontë, Emily, *Wuthering Heights* (London: Oxford University Press, 1957)
Conrad, Joseph, *Lord Jim* (London: Penguin, 2007)
Dickens, Charles, *A Tale of Two Cities* (London: Penguin, 2003)
Faulks, Sebastian, *Birdsong* (London: Vintage, 1994)
Gaiman, Neil, *The Graveyard Book* (London: Bloomsbury, 2008)
Golding, William, *Lord of the Flies* (London: Penguin, 1964)
Ishiguro, Kazuo, *Never Let Me Go* (London: Faber and Faber, 2010)
Magorian, Michelle, *Goodnight Mister Tom* (London: Puffin Books, 2011)
Ness, Patrick, *A Monster Calls* (London: Walker Books, 2012)
Pullman, Philip, *Northern Lights* (London: Scholastic, 1998)
Rees, Celia, *Witch Child* (London: Bloomsbury, 2009)
Shelley, Mary, *Frankenstein* (Chicago and London: The University of Chicago Press, 1982)
Steinbeck, John, *Of Mice and Men* (London: Penguin, 2006)
Stevenson, Robert Louis, *The Strange Case of Dr Jekyll and Mr Hyde* (New York: Signet Classics, 2012)
Stoker, Bram, *Dracula* (London: Penguin, 2003)

Plays
Bulwer-Lytton, Edward, *Richelieu: Or the Conspiracy* (South Yarra: Leopold Classic Library, 2009)
Shakespeare, William, *A Midsummer Night's Dream* (Oxford: Oxford University Press, 2009)
— *King Lear* (Oxford: Oxford University Press, 2013)
Macbeth (Oxford: Oxford University Press, 2009)
Measure for Measure (Oxford: Oxford University Press, 2013)
Romeo and Juliet (Oxford: Oxford University Press, 2008)
Twelfth Night (Oxford: Oxford University Press, 2010)
Williams, Tennessee, *A Streetcar Named Desire* (London: Penguin, 2009)

Poetry
Barrett Browning, Elizabeth, 'Mother and Poet' in *The Collected Poems of Elizabeth Barrett Browning* (Ware: Wordsworth, 2015)

Blake, William, 'Songs of Innocence and Experience' in *The Complete Poems* (London: Penguin, 1977)
Browning, Robert, 'Porphyria's Lover' in *Selected Poems* (London: Penguin, 2000)
Donne, John, 'Community' in *Selected Poems* (London: Penguin, 2006)
Eliot, T.S., 'The Waste Land' in *The Waste Land and Other Poems* (London: Faber and Faber, 2002)
Heaney, Seamus, 'Blackberry Picking' in *Death of a Naturalist* (London: Faber and Faber, 2006)
— 'Follower' in *Death of a Naturalist* (London: Faber and Faber, 2006)
Keats, John, 'To Autumn' in *Selected Poems* (London: Penguin, 2007)
— 'Ode to a Nightingale' in *Selected Poems* (London: Penguin, 2007)
Marvell, Andrew, 'To His Coy Mistress' in *The Complete Poems* (London: Penguin, 2005)
Mew, Charlotte, 'The Farmer's Bride' in *The Complete Poems* (London: Penguin, 2000)
Poe, Edgar Allan, 'The Raven' in *The Complete Poetry of Edgar Allan Poe* (New York: Signet, 2008)
Rossetti, Christina, 'Goblin Market' in *Selected Poems* (London: Penguin, 2008)
Shakespeare, William, 'Sonnet 18' in *The Complete Sonnets and Poems* (Oxford: Oxford University Press, 2008)
Sheers, Owen, 'Mametz Wood' in *Skirrid Hill* (Cardiff: Seren, 2005)
Stevenson, Robert Louis, 'Ballads' in *Selected Poems* (London: Penguin, 1998)
Taylor Coleridge, Samuel, 'The Rime of the Ancient Mariner' in *The Major Works* (Oxford: Oxford University Press, 2008)
Tennyson, Alfred, 'The Princess' in *Selected Poems* (London: Penguin, 2007)
— 'The Charge of the Light Brigade' in *Selected Poems* (London: Penguin, 2007)
Wolff, George, 'To my Wife' in *Loves and Dystopias: Poems* (Lulu, 2010)

Index

abstract nouns 22, 27–28, 34–35, 37, 114, 116
active voice 41–42, 46, 47, 51, 55, 56
adjectives 14, 26, 30, 35, 53, 54, 68, 79, 115
adverbs 54
alliteration 87, 111
anaphora 87
ancillary verbs 54
anthropomorphism 88
antimetabole 88
antithesis 88
assessment objectives 2, 3, 10, 92, 96, 103
assonance 88, 95
Austen, Jane: *Emma* 13–14; *Pride and Prejudice* 77–79
auxiliary verb 40

Barrett Browning, Elizabeth: 'Mother and Poet' 88
Blake, William: 'Songs of Innocence and Experience' 91, 109
Boyne, John: *The Boy in the Striped Pyjamas* 25–26, 30
brackets 75
Brontë, Charlotte: *Jane Eyre* 9–10
Brontë, Emily: *Wuthering Heights* 29
Browning, Robert: 'Porphyria's Lover' 37, 99, 100, 102–103
Bulwer-Lytton, Edward: *Richelieu: Or the Conspiracy* 90

caesura 88
capital letters 84
chiasmic structure 88
Coleridge, Samuel Taylor: 'The Rime of the Ancient Mariner' 91
colons 73

commas 71–73, 78, 81, 82
common nouns 21, 26, 27, 28, 30–31, 32, 33
complex sentences 4, 6, 9, 10, 13, 15, 17, 46, 115–116
compound adjectives 75
compound sentences 4, 6, 8, 9, 10, 11, 17, 47, 113, 115–116
concrete nouns 21, 33, 114, 115
conditional clause 5, 10, 43
conjunctions 10, 73
connotation 88, 96, 114
Conrad, Joseph: *Lord Jim* 91
consonance 89
context 9, 10, 37, 84, 106
continuous aspect 44–45
count nouns 22
creative writing 14–18, 30–31, 32–34, 50–52, 52–54, 54–56, 67–68, 81–84, 113, 114

dashes 75, 77, 82
declarative 6, 10, 17
definite determiners 67, 69
definitive article 60, 62, 64, 66,
demonstrative determiner 64, 65
demonstrative pronouns 24
demonstratives 61
determiners 26, 60–70, 113
Dickens, Charles: *A Tale of Two Cities* 87
differentiation 17, 33, 36, 54, 56, 70, 83, 85, 109, 113
direct speech 74
Donne, John: 'Community' 88

Elliot, T.S.: 'The Waste Land' 89
enjambment 89, 92–95, 111
epizeuxis 89, 101–102

exclamation marks 74, 78, 79
exclamatory 6–7, 8, 11, 12, 13–14, 17

Faulks, Sebastian: *Birdsong* 79–81
foreshadowing 8, 9, 11, 48
fricative 37
full stops 73, 74, 76–77, 79, 80–81
future perfect tense 40

Gaiman, Neil: *The Graveyard Book* 45–46
gerund 54
Golding, William: *Lord of the Flies* 47–48, 100, 114

half-rhyme 89
Heaney, Seamus: 'Blackberry Picking' 92, 93–94, 95, 97–98; 'Follower' 89
homophones 113
hyperbaton 89
hyperbole 89
hyphens 75

iambic pentameter 89
imagery 89, 105
imperative 6, 43, 48
indefinite article 60, 62, 64, 65, 66
indefinite determiners 67, 68
indefinite pronouns 25
independent clause *see* main clause
indicative 43, 46
infinitive 39, 40, 53
interrogative 7, 8, 11, 13–14, 17, 43, 61
interrogative pronouns 24
intransitive verbs 41, 46, 47, 51, 52, 54, 55, 56
inverted commas 74
Ishiguro, Kazuo: *Never Let Me Go* 63–65

Keats, John: 'Ode to a Nightingale' 91, 104, 105–106, 106–107, 110–111; 'To Autumn' 89
Kennedy, J F 88

lesson plans 16–18, 31–36, 68–70, 52–56, 82–85, 107–110

Magorian, Michelle: *Goodnight Mister Tom* 62
main clause 4–5, 6, 9, 11, 71, 72–73, 77, 81
main verb 40

Marvell, Andrew: 'To His Coy Mistress' 88
metaphor 31, 33, 90
metonym 110
metonymy 90, 104, 106
Mew, Charlotte: 'The Farmer's Bride' 37
modal verbs 40–41, 48, 49, 57–58
moods 43, 46

Ness, Patrick: *A Monster Calls* 76
non-count nouns 22
non-restrictive relative clause 5, 72
noun phrases 22, 60
nouns 21–38, 53, 54, 55, 60, 61, 113, 114, 115, 116

object pronouns 23
onomatopoeia 90
oxford comma 73
oxymoron 90

parallelism 91
participles 45
passive voice 40, 41–42, 46, 47, 51, 55, 56
past perfect tense 40, 48
pathetic fallacy 90, 99–101
perfective aspect 44, 53
personal pronouns 23
personification 90
phrasal verbs 42
play writing 19
Poe, Edgar Allen: 'The Raven' 87
Pope, Alexander: 'An Essay on Criticism' 91
possessive determiners 60–61, 62–63, 67, 68
possessive pronouns 24, 60, 68, 113
possessives 61
present continuous tense 40, 56
principal verb *see* main verb
pronouns 22–25, 27, 29–30, 38, 48, 116
proper nouns 21, 28, 30–31, 32
Pullman, Philip: *Northern Lights* 7–9
punctuation 9, 14, 15, 71–86, 114, 115

quantifying determiners 61
question marks 74, 79
quotation marks *see* inverted commas

Rees, Celia: *Witch Child* 31–34
reflexive pronouns 23

reflexive verbs 42, 47
relative clause 5, 72
relative pronoun 5, 24
repetition 101
reported speech 74
restrictive relative clause 5, 72
Rosetti, Christina: 'Goblin Market' 104–105

semi-colons 71, 72, 73, 78, 80, 81, 82
sentence construction 4–20, 46, 76–77, 80, 82, 115
Shakespeare 37–38, 112, 114
Shakespeare, William: *A Midsummer Night's Dream* 37; *Macbeth* 38, 57–8, 88, 89, 90, 99; *Measure for Measure* 89; *Romeo and Juliet* 89, 90; 'Sonnet' 18; *Twelfth Night* 89
Sheers, Owen: 'Mametz Wood' 92, 94–95, 96, 98
Shelley, Mary: *Frankenstein* 65–66
sibilance 37, 91
simile 30, 91
simple sentence 6, 8, 9, 11, 15, 17, 115–116
Steinbeck, John 91
Stevenson, Robert Louis: 'Ballads' 88
Stoker, Bram: *Dracula* 48–49

subject pronouns 23
subjunctive 43
subordinate clauses 4, 5, 6, 9, 15, 71, 73, 77
subordinate conjunction 5
syllogism 110
synaesthesia 91, 104–106
synecdoche 91, 110

Tennyson, Alfred: 'The Charge of the Light Brigade' 101; 'The Princess' 90
transitive verbs 41, 46, 47, 51, 52, 54, 55, 65
triadic structure 91

unseen texts 19, 37, 57, 115

verb tenses 43, 46, 48, 49, 53, 56, 57
verbs 15, 39–59, 113, 114, 115
volta 57
vowels 95

Williams, Tennessee: *A Streetcar Named Desire* 11–12
Wolff, George: 'To my Wife' 89

zoomorphism 91